Childcraft

THE HOW AND WHY LIBRARY

VOLUME 2

Time to Read

World Book, Inc.

a Scott Fetzer company

Chicago London Sydney Toronto

Acknowledgments

The publishers of *Childcraft—The How and Why Library* gratefully acknowledge the courtesy of the following publishers, agents, authors, and artists who have granted permission to use copyrighted material in this book. Any errors or omissions are unintentional and the publisher will be happy to make any necessary corrections in future printings. Full illustration acknowledgments for this volume appear on page 298.

Atheneum Publishers, Inc.: "When All the World Is Full of Snow" from *Hurry, Hurry Mary Dear! And Other Nonsense Poems* by N. M. Bodecker. Copyright © 1976 by N. M. Bodecker. A Margaret K. McElderry Book. Reprinted with the permission of Atheneum Publishers. "A Big Deal for the Tooth Fairy," "A Choosy Wolf," "In the Motel," and "My Dragon" from *The Phantom Ice Cream Man* by X. J. Kennedy. Copyright © 1979 by X. J. Kennedy. Illustration copyright © 1979 by David McPhail. A Margaret K. McElderry Book. Reprinted with the permission of Atheneum Publishers, Inc., and Curtis Brown, Ltd. "One Winter Night in August" from *One Winter Night in August* by X. J. Kennedy. Copyright © 1975 X. J. Kennedy. A Margaret K. McElderry Book. Reprinted with the permission of Atheneum Publishers, Inc., and Curtis Brown, Ltd. "Little Bits of Soft-Boiled Egg" from *A Child's Book of Manners* by Fay Maschler. Text copyright © 1978 Fay Maschler. Illustrations copyright © 1978 by Helen Oxenbury. Reprinted with the permission of Atheneum Publishers, Inc., and Jonathan Cape Ltd. "Bedtime Stories" from *See My Lovely Poison Ivy* by Lilian Moore. Copyright © 1975 by Lilian Moore. Picture copyright © 1975 by Diane Dawson. Reprinted with the permission of Atheneum Publishers. "Until I Saw the Sea" from *I Feel the Same Way* by Lilian Moore. Text copyright © 1967 by Lilian Moore. Illustration copyright © 1967 by Robert Quackenbush. Reprinted with the permission of Atheneum Publishers, Inc. "Mother Doesn't Want a Dog" and "Since Hanna Moved Away" from *If I Were in Charge of the World and Other Worries* by Judith Viorst. Text copyright © 1981 Judith Viorst. Reprinted with the permission of Atheneum Publishers, Inc. and Lescher & Lescher, Ltd.
Kenneth C. Bennett, Jr.: "End-of-Summer Poem" by Rowena Bastin Bennett. Reprinted by permission of the Estate of the author.
Marchette Chute: "Spring Rain" from *Around and About* by Marchette Chute. Copyright 1957 E. P. Dutton. Reprinted by permission of Mary Chute Smith.
The Connecticut Bank and Trust Company, N.A.: "Dogs and Weather" from *Skipping Along Alone* by Winifred Welles. By permission of the Connecticut Bank and Trust Company, N.A., agent for James Welles Shearer.
The Lois Lenski Covey Foundation, Inc.: "Sing a Song of People" from *The Life I Live* by Lois Lenski. Copyright © 1965 by The Lois Lenski Covey Foundation, Inc. Reprinted by permission of the Lois Lenski Covey Foundation, Inc.
Curtis Brown, Ltd.: "Girls Can, Too!" from *Girls Can, Too!* by Lee Bennett Hopkins. Text copyright © 1972 by Lee Bennett Hopkins. Reprinted by permission of Curtis Brown, Ltd. "J's the Jumping Jay Walker" from *All Around the Town* by Phyllis McGinley. The text copyright 1948 by Phyllis McGinley. Copyright renewed © 1976 by Phyllis McGinley. Reprinted by permission of Curtis Brown, Ltd.
Delacorte Press: "The Toaster" excerpted from the book *Laughing Time* by William Jay Smith. Copyright © 1953, 1955, 1956, 1957, 1959, 1968, 1974, 1977, 1980 by William Jay Smith. Reprinted by permission of Delacorte Press/Seymour Lawrence, and William Jay Smith.

Beatrice Schenk de Regniers: "Keep a Poem in Your Pocket" from *Something Special* by Beatrice Schenk de Regniers. Copyright © 1958 by Beatrice Schenk de Regniers. Reprinted by permission of the author.
Dodd, Mead & Company: "The Riddles" reprinted by permission of Dodd, Mead & Company, Inc., from *Morris and Boris: Three Stories* by Bernard Wiseman. Copyright © 1974 by Bernard Wiseman.
Doubleday & Company, Inc.: "If Once You Have Slept on an Island" from *Taxis and Toadstools* by Rachel Field. Copyright 1926 by The Century Company. Reprinted by permission of Doubleday, a division of Bantam, Doubleday, Dell Publishing Group, Inc. "Miss Norma Jean Pugh, First Grade Teacher" from *People I'd Like to Keep* by Mary O'Neill. Copyright © 1964 by Mary O'Neill. Reprinted by permission of Doubleday, a division of Bantam, Doubleday, Dell Publishing Group, Inc.
E. P. Dutton, Inc.: "Galoshes" from *Stories to Begin On* by Rhoda Bacmeister. Copyright 1940 by E. P. Dutton, Inc.; renewed 1968 by Rhoda Bacmeister. Reprinted by permission of the publisher. "The Family Dog" from *Tales of a Fourth Grade Nothing* by Judy Blume. Text copyright © 1972 by Judy Blume. Reprinted by permission of the publisher, E. P. Dutton, a division of NAL Penguin Inc. "The End" from *Now We Are Six* by A. A. Milne. Copyright 1927 by E. P. Dutton, renewed 1955 by A. A. Milne. Reprinted by permission of the publisher, E. P. Dutton, a division of NAL Penguin Inc., and The Canadian Publishers, McClelland and Stewart Limited, Toronto. "The Case of Merko's Grandson" and "The Case of the Bank Robber" from *Encyclopedia Brown, Boy Detective* by Donald J. Sobol. Copyright © 1963 by Donald J. Sobol. Reprinted by permission of the publisher, E. P. Dutton/Lodestar Books, a division of NAL Penguin Inc.
Kathleen Fraser: "Wrestling" from *Stilts, Somersaults, and Headstands,* © 1968. Reprinted by permission of the author.
Harcourt Brace Jovanovich, Inc.: "Questions at Night" from *Rainbow in the Sky* by Louis Untermeyer. Copyright 1935 by Harcourt Brace Jovanovich, Inc.; renewed 1963 by Louis Untermeyer. "The Opposite of Two" from *Opposites* by Richard Wilbur. Copyright © 1973 by Richard Wilbur. Reprinted by permission of Harcourt Brace Jovanovich, Inc.
Harper & Row, Publishers, Inc.: "First Snow" (text only) from *A Pocketful of Rhymes* by Marie Louise Allen. Copyright 1939 by Harper & Row, Publishers, Inc. Reprinted by permission of Harper & Row, Publishers, Inc. Complete text and 13 illustrations from *The Case of the Cat's Meow* by Crosby Bonsall. Copyright © 1965 by Crosby Bonsall. Reprinted by permission of Harper & Row, Publishers, Inc. Published in Great Britain by World's Work Ltd. "Rudolph Is Tired of the City" and "Vern" (text only) from *Bronzeville Boys and Girls* by Gwendolyn Brooks. Copyright © 1956 by Gwendolyn Brooks Blakely. Reprinted by permission of Harper & Row, Publishers, Inc. "Mummy Slept Late and Daddy Fixed Breakfast" and "How to Tell a Tiger" (text only) from *You Read to Me, I'll Read to You* by John Ciardi (J. B. Lippincott Company). Copyright © 1962 by John Ciardi. "Bedtime" and "The Night Will Never Stay" (text only) from *Poems for Children* by Eleanor Farjeon (J. B. Lippincott Company). Copyright 1933, 1961 by Eleanor Farjeon. Reprinted by permission of Harper & Row, Publishers, Inc., and Harold Ober Associates Incorporated. Text only of "June" from *Going Barefoot* by Aileen Fisher (Thomas Y. Crowell Company). Text copyright © 1960 by Aileen Fisher. Reprinted by permission of Harper & Row, Publishers, Inc. "Homework" and "Stupid Old Myself" (text only) from *Egg Thoughts and Other Frances Songs*
(continued on page 299)

Volume 2

Time to Read

Contents

About This Book

Time to Read is a collection of 21 stories and 129 poems and riddle rhymes selected to meet the needs and interests of two groups of children: young listeners and young readers.

A Note to Parents

For the preschooler, here are wonderful read-to picture books that you as a parent will enjoy as much as your listener. Imagine the smiles when your youngster discovers what baby mouse really wanted in Maria Polushkin's warm and loving tale, *Mother, Mother, I Want Another*. And don't forget to talk with your child about what is going on in Diane Dawson's lively and humorous illustrations.

Is your little one reluctant to take a bath? Then try reading about the antics of Harry in Gene Zion's *Harry the Dirty Dog*. Or, if you want to talk to your child about friendship, read the two stories about those good friends, Frog and Toad.

And don't overlook poems your youngster might enjoy, such as "My Nose," "Guess," "How to Tell a Tiger," "Table Manners," "Rules," "The Eensy, Weensy Spider," and "Bedtime Stories."

A Note to Young Readers

Time to Read gives you a chance to read some old favorites on your own—and to try out some new stories and poems, too. As you will discover, this book starts with stories that beginning readers will find easy to read and moves along to stories that are for more advanced readers.

Along the way, you will meet some wonderful storybook friends—Amelia Bedelia, Paddington Bear, Pippi Longstocking, and others. You will find out that some of their problems are much like your problems. Have you ever had a bad day such as Sam did in *I Should Have Stayed in Bed?* Or perhaps you have a younger brother or sister who is a pest like Fudge in "The Family Dog." And if you think you are smart, try matching wits with Encyclopedia Brown. By the way, don't skip the note at the end of each story. It will lead you to other stories you can find in the library.

Try the poems, too. For real fun, the humorous ones are hard to beat. And the serious ones will help you to see things in a different way.

So, turn the page—it's *Time to Read*!

Mother, Mother, I Want Another

by Maria Polushkin
pictures by Diane Dawson

It was bedtime in the mouse house. Mrs. Mouse took baby mouse to his room.

She helped him put on his pajamas and told him to brush his teeth.

She tucked him into his bed and read him a bedtime story.

She gave him a bedtime kiss, and then she said, "Good night."

But as she was leaving, baby
mouse started to cry. "Why are
you crying?" asked Mrs. Mouse.
"I want another, Mother."
"Another mother!" cried Mrs. Mouse.
"Where will I find another mother for my baby?"
Mrs. Mouse ran to get Mrs. Duck. "Please,
Mrs. Duck, come to our house and help put baby
mouse to bed. Tonight he wants another
mother."

Mrs. Duck came and
sang a song:

Quack, quack, mousie,
Don't you fret.
I'll bring you worms
Both fat and wet.

But baby mouse
said, "Mother, Mother,
I want another."

Mrs. Duck went to get Mrs. Frog. Mrs.
Frog came and sang:

Croak, croak, mousie,
Close your eyes.
I will bring you
Big fat flies.

But baby mouse said,
"Mother, Mother, I want
another."

Mrs. Frog went to get Mrs. Pig.

Mrs. Pig came and sang a song:

Oink, oink, mousie,
Go to sleep.
I'll bring some carrots
For you to keep.

But baby mouse said, "Mother, Mother,
I want another."

Mrs. Pig went to get Mrs. Donkey.

Mrs. Donkey came
and sang a song:

Hee-haw, mousie,
Hush-a-bye.
I'll sing for you
A lullaby.

But baby mouse
had had enough.

"NO MORE MOTHERS!"
he shouted.

"I want another
KISS."

"Really?"

"Well, now!"

"Indeed?"

"I see."

"Oh?"

Mrs. Duck
kissed baby
mouse.

Mrs. Frog kissed
baby mouse.

Mrs. Pig kissed
baby mouse.

And Mrs. Donkey
kissed baby mouse.

Then Mrs. Mouse gave baby mouse a drink of water. She tucked in his blanket. And she gave him a kiss.

Baby mouse smiled. "May I have another, Mother?"

"Of course," said Mrs. Mouse, and she leaned over and gave him *another* kiss.

Toucans Two
by Jack Prelutsky

Whatever one toucan can do
is sooner done by toucans two,
and three toucans (it's very true)
can do much more than two can do.

And toucans numbering two plus two can
manage more than all the zoo can.
In short, there is no toucan who can
do what four or three or two can.

Counting
by Karla Kuskin

To count myself
Is quickly done.
There's never more of me
Than one.

I Love You
author unknown

I love you, I love you,
I love you divine,
Please give me your bubble gum,
You're *sitting* on mine!

I Saw a Little Girl I Hate
by Arnold Spilka

I saw a little girl I hate
And kicked her with my toes.
She turned
And smiled
And KISSED me!
Then she punched me in the nose.

Happy Thought
by Robert Louis Stevenson

The world is so full of a number of things,
I'm sure we should all be as happy as kings.

Question
author unknown

Do you love me
Or do you not?
You told me once
But I forgot.

I Should Have Stayed in Bed

by Joan M. Lexau

Some days it doesn't pay to get up. Some
days you can't do anything right.

One day I woke up. The sun was shining.
Birds were singing.

I got dressed. I put on my shoes. I tied
the shoelaces. The shoes were on the wrong
feet.

When I untied the shoelaces, I made two

knots. So I left the shoes on the wrong feet. I went down to breakfast.

"Good morning, dear," said my mother. "Why are you wearing your Cub Scout suit? Tomorrow is Cub Scout day."

"Good morning, Sam," said my father. "Your shoes are on the wrong feet. What's the matter with you today? This isn't like you."

I got dressed all over again. When I tried to untie the shoelaces, they broke.

I put the shoes on the right feet. I went down again to breakfast.

"Not so much sugar on your cereal, dear," my mother said.

"I like it this way," I said. I put some more sugar on my cereal.

At the bottom it was all soggy sugar. I ate it all up. It was terrible.

I went to call for Albert. Good old Albert.
My best friend.

"Albert, hey, Albert," I yelled at his
window.

"Albert left. It's late," his mother said.

That Albert. Some friend!

I took off for school. I saw a nickel in the
street. "Good," I said. "Something good at last."

I went over to pick it up. My foot kicked
it into a sewer. "Boy, I should have stayed in
bed," I said.

I got to school when the first bell rang.

"Here comes Sam the snail," Albert said.
"What took you so long?"

I threw a notebook at him. He ducked.
The notebook hit Amy Lou.

"You could have killed me," Amy Lou said.
"I'm going to tell." She ran into the school.

I ran after her. "Amy Lou," I said. "Amy
Lou, Amy Lou, Amy Lou."

Amy Lou went into our room. "Sam tried
to kill me!" she yelled.

The teacher wasn't there. So everybody
ran around the room.

"Watch me," I said. "Watch how fast I

can go." I turned around and around and around, faster and faster.

The second bell rang. Everybody sat down. Everybody but me. I fell down.

The teacher came in. "Well, Sam?" said the teacher.

"I got dizzy," I said.

"Oh. Go see the nurse," said the teacher. So I did.

Boy, was the nurse mad when she found out why I got dizzy. She told me off. She gave me a note for my teacher.

The teacher told me off too. She told me to open my reader and read.

I read, "Bob walked down the dark

street. He was getting colder and colder. By and by he was a snowman."

Everybody laughed.

"He **saw** a snowman," said the teacher. "Maybe you are still dizzy, Sam. Amy Lou, it is your turn."

Amy Lou read it right. She always does.

Albert gave me a note. I opened it up.

The teacher saw it. "Read the note out loud," she said.

What could I do? I read it out loud. It said: "Can you read this fast? Eye yam. Eye yam. Eye ree lee yam. Eye man ut."

Everybody laughed.

I didn't look at Albert.

"You read that very well," said the teacher. "But after this when you and Albert have something to say, say it to all of us. No more notes."

I thought lunchtime would never come. But at last it did. I didn't wait for Albert.

"Sam, Albert is calling you," Amy Lou said.

"Albert?" I said. "Who is Albert? I don't know any Albert."

I ran all the way home. I said over and over, "I should have stayed in bed. I should have stayed in bed."

When I got home I said, "Why not? It can only help. Things can't get any worse."

So I went to my room. I put on my pajamas. I went to bed and counted to one hundred.

"I'll call the doctor," my mother said. "Now I know something is the matter."

"I'm all right," I said. "I'm starting the day over."

"Oh," said my mother. She looked at me as if I were crazy. But she didn't call the doctor.

I got up and put on my robe and slippers. I asked for some cereal. I put just a little sugar on it.

Then I got dressed and ran to school. I didn't see Albert. I heard the first bell ring. I

heard the second bell ring. Everybody was in
school.

No, not everybody. There was Albert by
the door.

"You're late," he said.

"Well, so are you," I said.

"I know," Albert said. "I saw you
coming, so I waited for you. We can both
stay after school."

Good old Albert. Good old best friend
Albert.

We went into our room.

"Sam and Albert are late," Amy Lou said.

"So I see," said the teacher.

"They'll have to stay after school, won't they?" said Amy Lou.

"Yes, they will," said the teacher.

"You know what?" said Amy Lou. "You know what? Sam has his slippers on!"

Everybody laughed. What a crazy day.

"Amy Lou," said the teacher, "you will have to stay after school. You talk too much."

I looked at Albert. Albert looked at me. It didn't look like such a bad day after all.

⚜

Would you like to read more about Sam and his best friend, Albert? Then follow them as they play detective in *The Rooftop Mystery*. Or, try another Joan Lexau book, *Benjie on His Own*. It's about a young boy who, even though he is afraid, does what he has to do.

I Woke Up
This Morning
by Karla Kuskin

I woke up this morning
At quarter past seven.
I kicked up the covers
And stuck out my toe.

And ever since then
(That's a quarter past seven)
They haven't said anything
Other than "no."

They haven't said anything
Other than "Please, dear,
Don't do what you're doing,"
Or "Lower your voice."

Whatever I've done
And however I've chosen,
I've done the wrong thing
And I've made the wrong choice.

I didn't wash well
And I didn't say thank you.
I didn't shake hands
And I didn't say please.

I didn't say sorry
When passing the candy.
I banged the box into
Miss Witelson's knees.

I didn't say sorry.
I didn't stand straighter.
I didn't speak louder
When asked what I'd said.

Well, I said
That tomorrow
At quarter past seven

They can
Come in and get me.

I'm Staying In Bed.

Throughout
the World

Throughout the world
Who is there like me?
Who is like me?
I touch the sky,
Indeed I touch the sky!

a Winnebago Indian song

My Nose
by Dorothy Aldis

It doesn't breathe;
It doesn't smell;
It doesn't feel
So very well.

I am discouraged
With my nose:
The only thing it
Does is blows.

Sick
by Shel Silverstein

"I cannot go to school today,"
Said little Peggy Ann McKay.
"I have the measles and the mumps,
A gash, a rash and purple bumps.
My mouth is wet, my throat is dry,
I'm going blind in my right eye.
My tonsils are as big as rocks,
I've counted sixteen chicken pox
And there's one more—that's seventeen,
And don't you think my face looks green?
My leg is cut, my eyes are blue—
It might be instamatic flu.
I cough and sneeze and gasp and choke,
I'm sure that my left leg is broke—
My hip hurts when I move my chin,
My belly button's caving in,
My back is wrenched, my ankle's sprained,
My 'pendix pains each time it rains.
My nose is cold, my toes are numb,
I have a sliver in my thumb.
My neck is stiff, my spine is weak,
I hardly whisper when I speak.
My tongue is filling up my mouth,
I think my hair is falling out.
My elbow's bent, my spine ain't straight,
My temperature is one-o-eight.
My brain is shrunk, I cannot hear,
There is a hole inside my ear.
I have a hangnail, and my heart is—what?
What's that? What's that you say?
You say today is . . . Saturday?
G'bye, I'm going out to play!"

Stupid Old Myself

by Russell Hoban

Stupid old myself today
Found a four-leaf clover,
Left it where it blew away,
All my good luck's over.
Done and finished, gone astray
Stupid old myself today.

Stupid with a brand-new kite
Lost it in a tree
Way up high and tangled tight—
No more kite for me.

Stupid falling off a log
When I tried to get
Close enough to catch a frog
Came home very wet.

Then I swapped my teddy bear
In a stupid muddle
For a doll that's lost her hair.
No more bear to cuddle.

Walking slowly and alone
Stupid and in sorrow
I just found a lucky stone—
Maybe I'll be smart tomorrow.
With today one day behind me
Maybe my good luck will find me.

Abu Ali: Three Tales of the Middle East

retold by Dorothy O. Van Woerkom

Abu Ali Counts His Donkeys

Abu Ali bought nine donkeys at the fair. He climbed on the first donkey. "Whr-r-r-r!" said Abu Ali. The donkey began to trot, and the other donkeys followed.

"Now," said Abu Ali, "are all my donkeys here?"

He turned around and counted. "One—two—three—four—five—six—seven—eight—EIGHT donkeys!"

Abu Ali jumped down from his donkey. He looked behind trees, behind bushes. No donkey.

"I will count again," he said. "One—two—three—four—five—six—seven—eight—nine—NINE donkeys!"

Abu Ali climbed back on his donkey. "Whr-r-r-r! Soon I will be home with my nine new donkeys."

CLIP, CLAPPETY-CLOP. CLIP, CLAPPETY-CLOP.

"Now how many donkeys do I have?"
Abu Ali counted EIGHT donkeys! He jumped
down from his donkey. He looked behind
rocks, over hilltops. No donkey. But when he
turned around—NINE donkeys!

"When I get home," said Abu Ali, "will I
have nine donkeys, or will I have eight?"

Abu Ali saw his friend Musa coming up
the road. "Help me, friend Musa!" he cried. "I
keep losing a donkey. Now I have nine. But

when I climb on my donkey—like this—I
have only eight donkeys!"

Musa laughed. "Eight donkeys? Nine
donkeys? Why, I see TEN donkeys."

"Ten donkeys?" said Abu Ali. "Where do
you see ten donkeys?"

"I see eight donkeys following your
donkey. I see the donkey you are sitting on."
Musa could not stop laughing.

"Oh!" said Abu Ali. "I am sitting on the
ninth donkey! But you said you see ten."

"The tenth donkey is the donkey sitting
on YOUR donkey," Musa said. "Its name is
Abu Ali!"

Abu Ali Fools His Friends

Three friends of Abu Ali told tall tales about how strong they were.

"But I am stronger than you are, Hamid," Abu Ali said, "and I am stronger than Musa or Nouri."

"Show us," said Nouri.

"Yes," said Musa. "What can you do?"

Abu Ali said, "I can stay out in the snow all night without heat or fire."

Musa laughed. So did Hamid and Nouri.

"But I can!" said Abu Ali. "If I can't, I will cook a fine dinner for you!"

So Abu Ali went out into the snow.

"Good night," said Hamid.

"Good luck," said Nouri.

"Don't freeze," Musa said.

The snow fell. The wind blew. Soon everyone but Abu Ali was asleep. How long the night was! How dark, and how cold!

Across the street, Abu Ali saw a candle
in a window. How bright it looked. How
warm and friendly. Abu Ali watched the
candle all night long. When the sun came up,
he went home to bed.

His friends came to wake him up. "Did
you do it?" Musa asked.

"Of course," said Abu Ali. "But I was happy
to see a candle in the house across the street."

"Oh?" Hamid said. "A candle gives out
heat!"

"You had heat?" said Nouri. "Then you
must cook our dinner!"

"All right, I will," said Abu Ali. And he
went into his kitchen.

The three friends waited . . . and waited. "Hurry, Ali! We are hungry," Musa said.

"I cannot hurry, Musa."

Hamid, Musa, and Nouri went to see why Abu Ali could not hurry. In the kitchen they saw a pot hanging from the ceiling. On the floor under the pot they saw a candle.

"If a candle gives out heat," said Abu Ali, "then SOMEDAY this candle will cook your dinner!"

Abu Ali Fools Himself

Abu Ali was going to Musa's house for dinner. On the way, he stopped to see Hamid. "Friend Hamid," he said, "may I wear your coat today?"

"Of course," said Hamid. "But why?"

"Because," said Abu Ali, "it has so many pockets."

Then Abu Ali went to Musa's house.

"Come in, Ali!" said Musa. "Sit down. Dinner is ready!"

"Thank you, Musa," said Abu Ali. He took some meat. "What fine meat," he said.

"Have some more," said Musa.

Abu Ali took another piece of meat. He put it in his pocket.

"Why did you do that?" Musa asked.

"My coat is hungry," Abu Ali said.

"Have some bread," said Musa.

Abu Ali took two loaves of bread. He put one loaf in a pocket.

"Is your coat still hungry?" asked Musa.

"Oh, yes," said Abu Ali. "This is a very hungry coat!"

Abu Ali took two bowls of rice. He took two figs, and two small cakes with icing. One of everything went into a pocket of the coat.

"Does your coat want some water?" Musa asked.

"No, thank you," said Abu Ali. "This coat is never thirsty."

When it was time to leave, Abu Ali said, "Good-by, Musa. Thank you for the fine dinner."

"Good-by, Ali," Musa said. "And good-by to your coat."

Abu Ali hurried home. "I will not cook tomorrow," he said. "My dinner is in these pockets." He put the coat on a hook and took a nap.

Hamid came by. "Friend Ali?" said Hamid. "I need my coat."

But Abu Ali was asleep. Hamid took his coat. It was heavy. "What a fine friend Ali is!" said Hamid. "I lend him my coat, and he fills my pockets with good things for me to eat!"

Dorothy Van Woerkom has retold other amusing folk tales. One, *Alexandra the Rock-Eater*, an old Romanian tale, is about a woman who must outwit a dragon to feed her one hundred children. You will also laugh at another of her stories, *Donkey Ysabel*, which is about a donkey whose position in the family is threatened by a new car.

Toot! Toot!

author unknown

A peanut sat on a railroad track,
His heart was all a-flutter;
The five-fifteen came rushing by—
Toot! toot! peanut butter!

Smart

by Shel Silverstein

My dad gave me one dollar bill
'Cause I'm his smartest son,
And I swapped it for two shiny quarters
'Cause two is more than one!

And then I took the quarters
And traded them to Lou
For three dimes—I guess he don't know
That three is more than two!

Just then, along came old blind Bates
And just 'cause he can't see
He gave me four nickels for my three dimes,
And four is more than three!

And I took the nickels to Hiram Coombs
Down at the seed-feed store,
And the fool gave me five pennies for them,
And five is more than four!

And then I went and showed my dad,
And he got red in the cheeks
And closed his eyes and shook his head—
Too proud of me to speak!

Algy Met a Bear

author unknown

Algy met a bear,
A bear met Algy.
The bear was bulgy,
The bulge was Algy.

Amelia Mixed the Mustard
by A. E. Housman

Amelia mixed the mustard,
    She mixed it good and thick;
She put it in the custard
    And made her Mother sick,
And showing satisfaction
    By many a loud huzza
"Observe," said she, "the action
    Of mustard on Mamma."

Man Is a Fool
author unknown

As a rule, man is a fool.
When it's hot, he wants it cool.
When it's cool, he wants it hot.
Always wanting what is not.

A Choosy Wolf
by X. J. Kennedy

"Why won't you eat me, wolf?" I asked.
"It wouldn't be much fun to.
Besides, I'm into natural foods
That nothing has been done to."

The Slithergadee
by Shel Silverstein

The Slithergadee has crawled out of the sea.
He may catch all the others, but he won't catch me.
No you won't catch me, old Slithergadee,
You may catch all the others, but you wo—

One Winter Night in August

by X. J. Kennedy

*How many things are
wrong with this story?*

One winter night in August
While the larks sang in their eggs,
A barefoot boy with shoes on
Stood kneeling on his legs.

At ninety miles an hour
He slowly strolled to town
And parked atop a tower
That had just fallen down.

He asked a kind old policeman
Who bit small boys in half,
"Officer, have you seen my pet
Invisible giraffe?"

"Why, sure, I haven't seen him."
The cop smiled with a sneer.
"He was just here tomorrow
And he rushed right back next year.

"Now, boy, come be arrested
For stealing frozen steam!"
And whipping out his pistol,
He carved some hot ice cream.

Just then a pack of dogfish
Who roam the desert snows
Arrived by unicycle
And shook the policeman's toes.

They cried, "Congratulations,
Old dear! Surprise, surprise!
You raced the worst, so you came in first
And you didn't win any prize!"

Then turning to the boyfoot bear,
They yelled, "He's overheard
What we didn't say to the officer!
(We never said one word!)

"Too bad, boy, we must turn you
Into a loathsome toad!
Now shut your ears and listen,
We're going to explode!"

But then, with an awful holler
That didn't make a peep,
Our ancient boy (age seven)
Woke up and went to sleep.

Frog and Toad

from *Frog and Toad Are Friends*
written and illustrated by Arnold Lobel

A Lost Button

Toad and Frog went for a long walk. They
walked across a large meadow. They walked
in the woods. They walked along the river. At
last they went back home to Toad's house.

"Oh, drat," said Toad. "Not only do my
feet hurt, but I have lost one of the buttons
on my jacket."

"Don't worry," said Frog. "We will go back to all the places where we walked. We will soon find your button."

They walked back to the large meadow. They began to look for the button in the tall grass.

"Here is your button!" cried Frog.

"That is not my button," said Toad. "That button is black. My button was white." Toad put the black button in his pocket.

A sparrow flew down. "Excuse me," said the sparrow. "Did you lose a button? I found one."

"That is not my button," said Toad. "That button has two holes. My button had four holes." Toad put the button with two holes in his pocket.

They went back to the woods and looked on the dark paths.

"Here is your button," said Frog.

"That is not my button," cried Toad.
"That button is small. My button was big."
Toad put the small button in his pocket.

A raccoon came out from behind a tree.
"I heard that you were looking for a button,"
he said. "Here is one that I just found."

"That is not my button!" wailed Toad.
"That button is square. My button was
round." Toad put the square button in his
pocket.

Frog and Toad went back to the river.
They looked for the button in the mud.

"Here is your button," said Frog.

"That is not my button!" shouted Toad.
"That button is thin. My button was thick."

Toad put the thin button in his pocket.
He was very angry. He jumped up and down
and screamed, "The whole world is covered
with buttons, and not one of them is mine!"

Toad ran home and slammed the door.
There, on the floor, he saw his white,
four-holed, big, round, thick button.

"Oh," said Toad. "It was here all the
time. What a lot of trouble I have made for
Frog."

Toad took all of the buttons out of his
pocket. He took his sewing box down from

the shelf. Toad sewed the buttons all over his jacket.

The next day Toad gave his jacket to Frog. Frog thought that it was beautiful. He put it on and jumped for joy. None of the buttons fell off. Toad had sewed them on very well.

A Swim

Toad and Frog went down to the river.

"What a day for a swim," said Frog.

"Yes," said Toad.

"I will go behind these rocks and put on my bathing suit."

"I don't wear a bathing suit," said Frog.

"Well, I do," said Toad. "After I put on
my bathing suit, you must not look at me
until I get into the water."

"Why not?" asked Frog.

"Because I look funny in my bathing
suit. That is why," said Toad.

Frog closed his eyes when Toad came out
from behind the rocks. Toad was wearing his
bathing suit. "Don't peek," he said.

Frog and Toad jumped into the water.
They swam all afternoon.

Frog swam fast and made big splashes.
Toad swam slowly and made smaller splashes.

A turtle came along the riverbank.

"Frog, tell that turtle to go away," said
Toad. "I do not want him to see me in my
bathing suit when I come out of the river."

Frog swam over to the turtle. "Turtle,"
said Frog, "you will have to go away."

"Why should I?" asked the turtle.

"Because Toad thinks that he looks
funny in his bathing suit, and he does not
want you to see him," said Frog.

Some lizards were sitting nearby. "Does
Toad really look funny in his bathing suit?"
they asked.

A snake crawled out of the grass. "If
Toad looks funny in his bathing suit," said
the snake, "then I, for one, want to see him."

"We want to see him too," said two dragonflies.

"Me too," said a field mouse. "I have not seen anything funny in a long time."

Frog swam back to Toad. "I am sorry, Toad," he said. "Everyone wants to see how you will look."

"Then I will stay right here until they go away," said Toad.

The turtle and the lizards and the snake and the dragonflies and the field mouse all

sat on the riverbank. They waited for Toad to
come out of the water.

"Please," cried Frog, "please go away!"
But no one went away.

Toad was getting colder and colder. He
was beginning to shiver and sneeze. "I will
have to come out of the water," said Toad. "I
am catching a cold."

Toad climbed out of the river. The water
dripped out of his bathing suit and down onto
his feet.

The turtle laughed. The lizards laughed.
The snake laughed. The field mouse laughed,
and Frog laughed.

"What are you laughing at, Frog?" said
Toad.

"I am laughing at you, Toad," said Frog,
"because you *do* look funny in your bathing
suit."

"Of course I do," said Toad. Then he
picked up his clothes and went home.

⚜

You can share more good times with these two friends in
Arnold Lobel's other books, *Days with Frog and Toad*
and *Frog and Toad Together*. And if you would like to
learn about real frogs and toads, and how to tell them
apart, try *The Toad Hunt* by Janet Chenery.

Wrestling
by Kathleen Fraser

I like wrestling with Herbie because
he's my best friend.
We poke each other
(but not very hard)
and punch each other
(but not very hard)
and roll on the grass
and pretend to have fights
just to make our sisters scream.
But sometimes if he hits me too much
and it hurts,
I get mad
and I punch him back
as hard as I can
and then we both are crying
and going into our houses
and slamming our back doors on each other.
But the next day, if it's sunny,
we come out into our yards
and grin at each other,
and sometimes he gives me an apple
or I give him a cookie and
then we start wrestling again.

The Opposite of Two
by Richard Wilbur

What is the opposite of *two?*
A lonely me, a lonely you.

Whispers
by Myra Cohn Livingston

Whispers
   tickle through your ear
   telling things you like to hear.
Whispers
   are as soft as skin
   letting little words curl in.
Whispers
   come so they can blow
   secrets others never know.

Since Hanna Moved Away
by Judith Viorst

The tires on my bike are flat.
The sky is grouchy gray.
At least it sure feels like that
Since Hanna moved away.

Chocolate ice cream tastes like prunes.
December's come to stay.
They've taken back the Mays and Junes
Since Hanna moved away.

Flowers smell like halibut.
Velvet feels like hay.
Every handsome dog's a mutt
Since Hanna moved away.

Nothing's fun to laugh about.
Nothing's fun to play.
They call me, but I won't come out
Since Hanna moved away.

People
by Charlotte Zolotow

Some people talk and talk
and never say a thing.
Some people look at you
and birds begin to sing.

Some people laugh and laugh
and yet you want to cry.
Some people touch your hand
and music fills the sky.

The Case of
the Cat's Meow

by Crosby Bonsall
illustrations by Crosby Bonsall

Snitch was yelling. He was pulling a wagon
with a funny thing in it. And he was yelling.

"Stop yelling," yelled his brother, Wizard.

"Stop yelling," yelled his friend Skinny.

"Stop yelling," yelled his friend Tubby.

Snitch stopped yelling. It was very quiet.

The little noise in the wagon sounded
like a loud cry.

"MEOW!"

There, in an old bird cage, sat Mildred.
Mildred was Snitch's cat. "I'm keeping her
safe," Snitch said. "Somebody might steal
her."

"Who wants old Mildred?" Tubby said.
"She's dumb."

"She's no fun," Skinny said.

"She makes too much noise," Wizard
said.

"She's nice!" Snitch yelled. "I love
Mildred!"

"Nobody is going to steal Mildred,"
Wizard said. "We are private eyes. We have
our own clubhouse. We have a sign on the

door. Nobody will steal anything. Take my word for it."

"We can catch anybody now," Tubby said. "We have an alarm."

"What alarm?" Snitch asked.

"The alarm we just put in," Skinny said. "Step over this string."

"See," Wizard said, "if anybody comes sneaking around here, he will trip over this string. That will pull this pail of water down on his head. Then the string on the pail handle will ring this bell."

"And it will ring and ring and ring," Snitch cried. "And we will catch whoever wants to steal Mildred."

"Nobody wants to steal Mildred," Wizard said. "Take my word for it."

Snitch started to yell.

"Come on," said Wizard. "It's almost time for supper."

"I knew it must be," Tubby said.

They stepped over the string. Nobody wanted to set off the alarm.

When Snitch and Wizard got home, Mildred ran up the back steps. She ran in the little door in the big door that was her door.

59

"She's nice," Snitch said. "I love
Mildred."

But did Mildred love Snitch? The next
morning she didn't come when Snitch called
her. He called and called and called.

Wizard looked out the window.

"Somebody stole Mildred," Snitch yelled.

"Nobody stole Mildred," Wizard said.
"Take my word for it." But he came down in
a hurry.

"I'll call Skinny and Tubby," Wizard said.
"They will help us find Mildred."

"Somebody stole her," Snitch said. And
he started to yell.

The boys looked for Mildred all that day.

"Anybody seen a dumb cat?" Tubby asked.

"Anybody seen a cat?" Skinny asked. "She doesn't do much."

"Anybody seen a noisy cat?" Wizard asked.

"Have you seen my cat Mildred?" Snitch asked. "She's soft and she's nice. And I love her."

But he did not find Mildred. Nobody found Mildred. Nobody had even seen Mildred.

Back at the clubhouse Wizard said, "We are not very good private eyes if we can't find Mildred."

"But how can we?" Skinny asked.

"Food!" Tubby said. "Mildred has to eat."

"That's a good idea," said Wizard.
"Tonight we'll put food in the yard. If
Mildred is hungry, she'll come home."

"She likes liver," Snitch said, "and
strawberry jelly. Without seeds."

"*I* like strawberry jelly," Tubby said.

Each of the boys brought some food.
Next day they had cats, all right.

They had cats in the tree, cats on the

roof. They had cats on the grass and one cat
sitting on a stone in the middle of the brook.
But no Mildred.

"Our plan was no good," Wizard said.
"How do we get rid of these cats?"

"I know!" Skinny cried. "Dogs! Dogs will
chase the cats away."

"They will scare Mildred," Snitch said.

"Mildred isn't here," Wizard said.

Snitch started to yell again.

The boys brought every dog they could
find on the block. They got rid of the cats, all
right. But now they had dogs.

They had dogs in the tree, dogs on the

roof. They had dogs on the grass and one dog sitting on a stone in the middle of the brook. And it took the rest of the day to take the dogs home.

After supper Wizard called a meeting. "We have to keep our eyes open day and night," he said. "Let's ask if we can sleep in the yard tonight."

They went to bed even before their bedtime. They liked being outdoors. It was warm. The sky was full of stars. Soon each of them was sound asleep. And that was when the alarm went off.

The bell rang and rang. Wizard was up first. And then Skinny. Tubby got stuck in his sleeping bag. So he took it with him. Wizard turned on his flashlight. There was Snitch.

"I heard someone stealing Mildred," he said.

"You can't steal a cat who is not here!" Wizard yelled.

But they all went into the house for the rest of the night.

Next day Snitch told them something. "Last night I put food in Mildred's dish. And now it's gone!"

Wizard was mad because he had not thought of Mildred's dish. But he had a plan. That night he put Mildred's dish on a cookie tin filled with flour. "Whoever is eating the food will have to walk over the flour."

"And the white feet will leave a trail we can follow," Skinny cried.

Next morning the food was gone. But there were clear white paw prints going down the steps. Then the paw prints stopped.

"Shucks," Tubby cried, "the flour didn't last long enough."

And Snitch started to yell.

"What will we do now?" Skinny asked.

"Try again tonight," Wizard said. "And we will lock Mildred's door."

"Why?" asked Tubby.

"That cat is so noisy," Wizard said, "she will cry if she can't get in."

"And we'll hear her," Tubby said. "And the case will be solved."

"Then we'll be private ears," Skinny said.

That night the boys met on the porch. "Now let's keep our eyes open," Wizard said.

They went to bed early. But the night was warm and the sky was full of stars. Soon they were sound asleep.

"MEOW!"

"What was that?" Tubby whispered.

"Just an old cat," Snitch said. He started to go back to sleep. "A CAT!" he shouted. "It's Mildred! She is found!"

Wizard turned on his flashlight. It was

Mildred, all right. But she was going away.
"Meow," she said as she left.

"Follow that cat," Wizard yelled.

Down the steps they ran, over the grass,
up to the clubhouse. Mildred was one jump
ahead of them. One more jump took her over
the string. The string that was part of the
alarm.

"Some alarm!" Wizard said. "It sure
doesn't catch cats!"

Each boy stepped over the string. Mildred
jumped into the basket in the corner.

"Where's Mildred?" cried Snitch. "I brought her supper."

"The case is solved," said Wizard. "I told you nobody stole her."

Snitch ran over to the basket. He started
to yell again. "MILDRED HAS KITTENS!"

"Oh, boy, I want one," Tubby cried.

"Me too," said Skinny.

"Don't forget me," Wizard said.

But Snitch had his arms around the
basket. "Tubby said Mildred was dumb,"
Snitch said. "Skinny said she was no fun.
Wizard said she made too much noise."

Well, they *had* said all those things. Right then they changed their minds. Mildred was nice. They loved her.

And so they waited for the kittens to grow old enough to leave their mother.

When they were old enough, Snitch gave a kitten to each private eye.

"This is one case I'm glad we solved," Skinny said.

"It's lucky," said Tubby, "we're such good private eyes. The alarm didn't help us."

"Snitch was the only one we ever caught with it," Wizard said.

"Mildred will take care of us now," Snitch said.

"No, *my* cat will," said Tubby.

"No, *my* cat will," said Skinny.

"No, *my* cat will," said Wizard. "You can take my word for it."

And Snitch was yelling again.

⚜

You can join Wizard and his friends in other books by Crosby Bonsall. Discover how they solve such mysteries as *The Case of the Dumb Bells* and *The Case of the Hungry Stranger*—or see them outwitted by Marigold and her friends in *The Case of the Double Cross*.

Guess

by John Ciardi

ONE is a creeper and sleepy in his shell.
TWO is a hopper and he hops very well.
THREE is a flopper and his flippers flap.
FOUR is a jumper with a jump-in lap.
FIVE is a drinker with a dip-in nose.
SIX is a dipper with flippers on his toes.
SEVEN is a tapper with a tripper in his beak.
EIGHT is a nutter with a nut-sack in his cheek.
NINE is a hanger with a banger in his head.
TEN is The Stopper who stepped in and said:
"It's time for the guessing. Here in a line
Are all the numbers from one to nine.
Now look about you, and right or wrong
Guess, if you can, where they belong."

How to Tell a Tiger

by John Ciardi

People who know tigers
  Very very well
All agree that tigers
  Are not hard to tell.

The way to tell a tiger is
  With lots of room to spare.
Don't try telling them up close
  Or we may not find you there.

I Asked My Mother

author unknown

I asked my mother for fifty cents
To see the elephant jump the fence.
He jumped so high that he touched the sky
And never came back till the Fourth of July.

The Ostrich Is a Silly Bird

by Mary E. Wilkins Freeman

The ostrich is a silly bird
  With scarcely any mind.
He often runs so very fast,
  He leaves himself behind.

And when he gets there, has to stand
  And hang about til night,
Without a blessed thing to do
  Until he comes in sight.

Miss Norma Jean Pugh,
First Grade Teacher

by Mary O'Neill

Full of oatmeal
And gluggy with milk
On a morning in springtime
Soft as silk
When legs feel slow
And bumblebees buzz
And your nose tickles from
Dandelion fuzz
And you long to
Break a few
Cobwebs stuck with
Diamond dew
Stretched right out
In front of you—
When all you want
To do is *feel*
Until it's time for
Another meal,
Or sit right down
In the cool
Green grass
And watch the
Caterpillars pass....

Who cares if
Two and two
Are four or five
Or red or blue?
Who cares whether
Six or seven
Come before or after
Ten or eleven?
Who cares if
C-A-T
Spells cat or rat
Or tit or tat
Or ball or bat?
Well, I do
But I didn't
Used to—
Until MISS NORMA JEAN PUGH!
She's terribly old
As people go
Twenty-one-or-five-or-six
Or so
But she makes a person want to
KNOW!

The End
by A. A. Milne

When I was One,
I had just begun.

When I was Two,
I was nearly new.

When I was Three,
I was hardly Me.

When I was Four,
I was not much more.

When I was Five,
I was just alive.

But now I am Six,
    I'm clever as clever.
So I think I'll be six now
    for ever and ever.

The Riddles

from *Morris and Boris*
by Bernard Wiseman

Boris the Bear met Morris the Moose.

"Do you like riddles?" Boris asked.

Morris asked, "How do they taste?"

Boris said, "You do not eat riddles."

Morris asked, "Do you drink them?"

Boris said, "You do not eat riddles. You do not drink riddles. You ask them. Listen—I will ask you a riddle."

Boris asked, "What has four feet..."

Morris yelled, "ME!"

"I did not finish," Boris said. "What has four feet and a tail..."

"ME!" Morris yelled.

"I still did not finish!" Boris cried. "Let me finish!"

Morris put a hoof over his mouth.

Boris asked, "What has four feet and a tail and flies?"

"ME!" Morris yelled. "I have four feet and a tail, and flies come and sit on me all the time!"

"No, no!" Boris growled. "The answer is: a horse in an airplane!

"Here is another riddle. What kind of comb cannot comb hair?"

"I know!" Morris cried. "A broken comb!"

"NO! NO! NO!" Boris shouted. "The answer is: a honeycomb!"

"What is a honeycomb?" Morris asked.

Boris said, "It is a bee house. Don't you know anything?"

Morris said, "I know about riddles. You do not eat riddles. You do not drink riddles. You ASK riddles."

Boris said, "And you must answer them! Try to answer this riddle. What kind of bee does not sting?"

"I know!" cried Morris. "A friendly bee!"

"NO! NO!" Boris yelled.

Morris cried, "A sleeping bee!"

"NO! NO! NO!" Boris shouted. "The answer is: a beetle. Oh, you don't know how to answer riddles. I am not going to ask you any more."

Morris said, "You know how to answer riddles. Let me ask you riddles."

"Go ahead," said Boris. "Ask me riddles."

Morris asked, "What has four feet and a tail and flies?"

Boris answered, "A horse in an airplane."

"No! No!" Morris cried. "A moose in an airplane!"

Boris yelled, "You mean a HORSE!"

Morris said, "I mean a moose. I want a moose to get an airplane ride!"

Then Morris said, "Here is another riddle. What kind of comb cannot comb hair?"

Boris said, "A honeycomb."

"No! No! No!" Morris cried. "The answer is: a bee comb."

Boris asked, "What is a bee comb?"

Morris said, "The comb a bee uses. It cannot comb hair. A bee has no hair!"

Boris shouted, "Oh, you don't know anything about riddles! I am going home!"

A bird asked Morris, "What is he angry about?"

"Riddles," said Morris. "He does not like them."

❧

You can join Morris and Boris in many other funny adventures in *Morris Has a Cold* and *Morris Goes to School*, both by Bernard Wiseman. And if you enjoy riddles, try *Ji-Nongo-Nongo Means Riddles* by Verna Aardema, which is a collection of African "riddles," some funny and some that are wise observations on life. But if it's "instant" riddles you want, just turn the page.

A Riddle! A Riddle!

1. Riddle me, riddle me, what is that,
   Over the head and under the hat?

2. There's a flower in the garden,
   It's just like a cup;
   It's yellow, as yellow as butter,
   And they call it _____.

3. A riddle, a riddle, as I suppose,
   a hundred eyes and never a nose.

4. Old Mother Twitchett had but one eye,
   And a long tail, which she left fly;
   And every time she went over a gap,
   She left a bit of her tail in a trap.

5. Long legs and crooked thighs,
   Little head and no eyes.

1. hair
2. a buttercup
3. a potato
4. a needle and thread
5. a pair of tongs

1. A house full, a hole full,
   And you cannot gather a bowl full.

2. Black within and red without,
   With four corners round about.

3. Red within and red without,
   With four corners round about.

4. From house to house he goes,
   A messenger small and slight;
   And whether it rains or snows,
   He sleeps outside in the night.

5. Higher than a house,
   Higher than a tree;
   Oh, whatever can that be?

1. smoke or mist
2. a chimney
3. a brick
4. a lane
5. a star

1. First they dress in green,
    Then they change to brown;
    And some will even wear
    A red or golden gown!

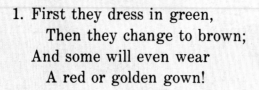

2. Four stiff-standers,
    Four dilly-danders,
    Two lookers, two crookers,
    And a long wiggle-waggle.

3. Runs all day and never walks,
    Often murmurs, never talks;
  It has a bed and never sleeps;
    It has a mouth and never eats.

1. leaves
2. a cow
3. a river

1. Little Nancy Etticoat,
   With a white petticoat,
   And a red nose;
   She has no feet or hands,
   The longer she stands
   The shorter she grows.

2. Twelve little figures around me,
     One pale face to guard;
   Two hands crossed on my fair white breast
     Can you guess me? I am not hard.

3. Two brothers we are, great burdens we bear,
    On which we are bitterly pressed;
  The truth is to say, we are full all the day,
    And empty when we go to rest.

1. a candle
2. a clock
3. a pair of shoes

1. Two legs sat upon three legs
   With one leg in his lap;
   In comes four legs
   And runs away with one leg;
   Up jumps two legs,
   Catches up three legs,
   Throws it after four legs,
   And makes him bring back one leg.

2. As I was going to St. Ives,
   I met a man with seven wives,
   Each wife had seven sacks,
   Each sack had seven cats,
   Each cat had seven kits:
   Kits, cats, sacks, and wives,
   How many were there going to St. Ives?

1. "Two legs" is a man, "three legs" is a stool, "four legs" is a dog, and "one leg" is a leg of lamb.

2. One or none, depending upon how the question is read.

Harry the Dirty Dog

by Gene Zion

Harry was a white dog with black spots who
liked everything, except ... getting a bath. So
one day when he heard the water running in
the tub, he took the scrubbing brush ... and
buried it in the backyard. Then he ran away
from home.

He played where they were fixing the street and got very dirty.

He played at the railroad and got even dirtier.

He played tag with other dogs and became dirtier still.

He slid down a coal chute and got the dirtiest of all.

In fact, he changed from a white dog with black spots, to a black dog with white spots.

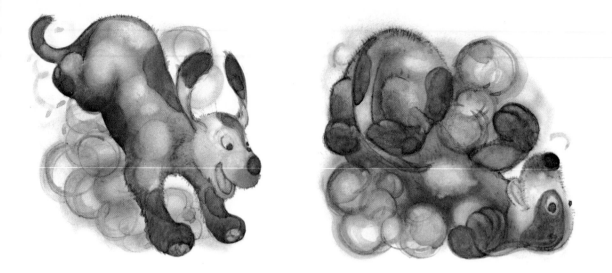

Although there were many other things
to do, Harry began to wonder if his family
thought that he had *really* run away.

He felt tired and hungry too, so without
stopping on the way he ran back home.

When Harry got to his house, he crawled
through the fence and sat looking at the back
door.

One of the family looked out and said,
"There's a strange dog in the backyard . . . by
the way, has anyone seen Harry?"

When Harry heard this, he tried very
hard to show them *he* was Harry. He started
to do all his old, clever tricks. He flip-flopped
and he flop-flipped. He rolled over and played
dead. He danced and he sang.

He did these tricks over and over again,

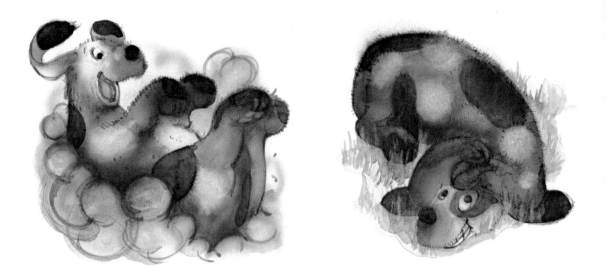

but everyone shook his head and said, "Oh, no, it couldn't be Harry."

Harry gave up and walked slowly toward the gate, but suddenly he stopped.

He ran to a corner of the garden and started to dig furiously. Soon he jumped away from the hole barking short, happy barks.

He'd found the scrubbing brush! And carrying it in his mouth, he ran into the house. Up the stairs he dashed, with the family following close behind.

He jumped into the bathtub and sat up begging, with the scrubbing brush in his mouth, a trick he certainly had never done before.

"This little doggie wants a bath!" cried the little girl, and her father said, "Why don't you and your brother give him one?"

Harry's bath was the soapiest one he'd

ever had. It worked like magic. As soon as the children started to scrub, they began shouting, "Mummy! Daddy! Look, look! Come quick! It's Harry! It's Harry! It's Harry!" they cried.

Harry wagged his tail and was very, very happy. His family combed and brushed him lovingly, and he became once again a white dog with black spots.

It was wonderful to be home. After dinner, Harry fell asleep in his favorite place, happily dreaming of how much fun it had been getting dirty. He slept so soundly, he didn't even feel the scrubbing brush he'd hidden under his pillow.

⚜

Did you enjoy meeting Harry? If so, you can join him on other adventures in *Harry and the Lady Next Door*, *Harry by the Sea*, and *No Roses for Harry*, all by Gene Zion.

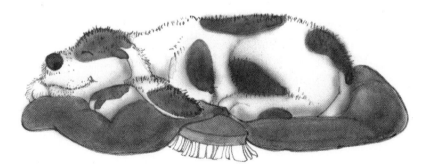

Mother Doesn't Want a Dog

by Judith Viorst

Mother doesn't want a dog.
Mother says they smell,
And never sit when you say sit,
Or even when you yell.
And when you come home late at night
And there is ice and snow,
You have to go back out because
The dumb dog has to go.

Mother doesn't want a dog.
Mother says they shed,
And always let the strangers in
And bark at friends instead,
And do disgraceful things on rugs,
And track mud on the floor,
And flop upon your bed at night
And snore their doggy snore.

Mother doesn't want a dog.
She's making a mistake.
Because, more than a dog, I think
She will not want this snake.

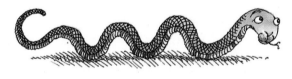

Dogs and Weather

by Winifred Welles

I'd like a different dog
    For every kind of weather—
A narrow greyhound for a fog,
    A wolfhound strange and white,
With a tail like a silver feather
    To run with in the night,
When snow is still, and winter stars are bright.

In the fall I'd like to see
    In answer to my whistle,
A golden spaniel look at me.
    But best of all for rain
A terrier, hairy as a thistle,
    To trot with fine disdain
Beside me down the soaked, sweet-smelling lane.

Vern

by Gwendolyn Brooks

When walking in a tiny rain
Across the vacant lot,
A pup's a good companion—
If a pup you've got.

And when you've had a scold,
And no one loves you very,
And you cannot be merry,
A pup will let you look at him,
And even let you hold
His little wiggly warmness—

And let you snuggle down beside.
Nor mock the tears you have to hide.

Galoshes

by Rhoda W. Bacmeister

Susie's galoshes
Make splishes and sploshes
And slooshes and sloshes,
As Susie steps slowly
Along in the slush.

They stamp and they tramp
On the ice and concrete,
They get stuck in the muck and the mud;
But Susie likes much best to hear

The slippery slush
As it slooshes and sloshes,
And splishes and sploshes,
All round her galoshes!

The Muddy Puddle
by Dennis Lee

I am sitting
In the middle
Of a rather Muddy
Puddle,
With my bottom
Full of bubbles
And my rubbers
Full of Mud,

While my jacket
And my sweater
Go on slowly
Getting wetter
As I very
Slowly settle
To the Bottom
Of the Mud.

And I find that
What a person
With a puddle
Round his middle
Thinks of mostly
In the muddle
Is the Muddi-
Ness of Mud.

Mud
by Polly Chase Boyden

Mud is very nice to feel
All squishy-squash between the toes!
I'd rather wade in wiggly mud
Then smell a yellow rose.

Nobody else but the rosebush knows
How nice mud feels
Between the toes.

Teach Us,
Amelia Bedelia

by Peggy Parish

The telephone was ringing.

"I'm coming, I'm coming," said Amelia
Bedelia. She answered the telephone. "Mrs.
Rogers!" she said. "Where are you?"

"I'm at the airport in Pinewood," said
Mrs. Rogers.

"You didn't tell me you were going
away," said Amelia Bedelia.

"I'm not," said Mrs. Rogers. "I'm
meeting the new teacher. But her plane is
late."

"That's too bad," said Amelia Bedelia.

"The telephone at the school is out of order," Mrs. Rogers went on. "Please go to Mr. Carter's office at the school. Tell him what I said."

"I'll go right now," said Amelia Bedelia.

Amelia Bedelia got her things. She walked to school. "Where is Mr. Carter's office?" she asked.

"That first door," said a child.

Amelia Bedelia walked in. "Mrs. Rogers tried to call you," she said. "But your telephone is out of order."

"I know," said Mr. Carter. "But thank goodness you're here. The children are going wild. Miss Lane left a list for today. I'll take you to the room." He handed Amelia Bedelia the list. "Follow me," he said.

They went down the hall. Mr. Carter opened a door. Children were all over the place.

"All right," said Mr. Carter. "Quiet! This is your new teacher."

"Me! Teach!" said Amelia Bedelia. But Mr. Carter was gone. She looked at the children. They looked at her. "I'm Amelia Bedelia," she said.

The children giggled.

"You're nice," said Amelia Bedelia. "I do like happy children. But we have a lot to do." She held up the list. "We must do just what this says," she said. "Now, what's first?"

Amelia Bedelia read, " 'Call the roll.' " She looked puzzled. "Call the roll! What roll?" she said. "Does anybody have a roll?"

"I have," said Peter.

"Do get it," said Amelia Bedelia.

Peter opened his lunch box. "Here it is," he said.

"Now I have to call it," said Amelia

Bedelia. "Roll! Hey, roll! All right, that takes care of that."

The children roared.

Amelia Bedelia read her list. "Land sakes," she said. "Listen to this. 'Sing a song,' I never was much of a hand at singing. But it says sing a song. So I'll sing." And she did!

"More! More!" shouted the children. "No," said Amelia Bedelia. "It said *a* song. I did just that."

"Ahh," said the children.

"Now it's reading time," said Amelia Bedelia. "I know about that. I read my cookbook. It tells me just what to do."

She held up a book. She said, "Is this the right one?"

"Yes," said Amanda.

Amelia Bedelia opened the book. "I declare," she said. "This is a good one. Are you ready?"

"Yes," said the children.

"All right," said Amelia Bedelia. "It says, 'Run, run, run.' "

The children just sat.

Amelia Bedelia clapped her hands. "Run," she said. "Run, run, run."

Amelia Bedelia ran. The children ran
after her. Around the room, through the halls,
around the block they ran. Finally they ran
back into the room.

Amelia Bedelia plopped on her chair.
"That takes care of run, run, run," she said.
"Your book plumb tired me out. Let's see
what's next. I hope we don't have to run to
do it." She looked at the list.

She said, "It's science time. Each of you
should plant a bulb. Do you know about
that?"

"Yes," said Tim. "We brought our pots."

"Where are the bulbs?" said Amelia
Bedelia.

"In the top closet," said Rebecca. "Miss
Lane said so."

Amelia Bedelia looked and looked.
"Nothing here but some dried-up onions," she

said. "You all go outside. Put some soil in your pots. I'll go buy some bulbs."

Amelia Bedelia went to the store. She hurried back. The children were waiting.

"Here's a bulb for you and you," said Amelia Bedelia. She gave everybody a bulb.

The children looked surprised. Then they

started giggling. But they planted those bulbs. They put the pots on the window sill.

"Those do look right pretty," said Amelia Bedelia. "And I learned something new. I didn't know you could plant bulbs."

Suddenly a bell rang. "What's that for?" said Amelia Bedelia.

"Free time," yelled the children.

"Good," said Amelia Bedelia.

The children ran outside. Amelia Bedelia sat down to rest.

Then free time ended. Back came the children.

"It's quiet time now," said Amelia Bedelia. "You're supposed to read stories."

Each child chose a book. All was quiet.

"Why aren't you reading?" said Amelia Bedelia.

"We are," said Ed.

"I don't hear you," said Amelia Bedelia.

The children looked at Amelia Bedelia. They looked at each other.

And Amelia Bedelia heard them all right.
"My, I'll be glad when quiet time is over,"
she said. "My ears hurt."

Jeff said, "Art comes next. That's fun."

Amelia Bedelia looked at her list. "You're
right," she said. "You must paint pictures now."

The children got sheets of art paper.

"What are you doing?" said Amelia Bedelia.

"We're going to paint pictures," said Bud.

"But how can you?" said Amelia Bedelia.
"There's no picture there to paint."

"We'll make pictures," said Mary.

"Oh no!" said Amelia Bedelia. "This says
to paint pictures. You can't paint a picture
without a picture to paint. Better find one
for yourselves."

The children ran around the room. Not a picture was left on the wall. But all the children were painting. Soon the pictures were back on the wall.

"They sure look different," said Steve.

"Yes," said Amelia Bedelia. "Mr. Carter will be surprised."

The children shook their heads.

"He sure will," said Janet.

"What's next?" said Jamie.

"Our play," said Rebecca. "We have to practice our play."

"Practice play!" said Amelia Bedelia. "You mean children have to practice play? School sure has changed since I went. All right, out you go."

"But Amelia Bedelia," said the children.

"No buts," said Amelia Bedelia. "Let's go. Start playing. Practice that jumping rope some more," said Amelia Bedelia. "I can do better than that."

"Show us," said Janet.

And Amelia Bedelia did.

"I can run faster than that," said Amelia Bedelia.

"Show us," said Steve.

So Amelia Bedelia did.

"That's fine," she said. "You've practiced long enough. Let's go inside. Let me see what's next," said Amelia Bedelia. "Here are some problems for you."

"Yuck!" said the children.

"Ginny, get your apples," said Amelia Bedelia.

"What apples?" said Ginny.

Amelia Bedelia looked puzzled. She said, "But it says Ginny has four apples. Paul takes away two. Oops," said Amelia Bedelia. "I don't think I was supposed to tell that part."

She read the other problems. "These all have apples in them," she said. "Does anybody have apples?" The children shook their heads.

Then Amelia Bedelia had an idea. "Let's go to my house," she said. "We have lots of apples."

"Yes!" shouted the children.

"We better leave a note," said Amelia Bedelia. She went to the blackboard and wrote, "We are at the Rogers' house."

Then off they went to the Rogers' backyard.

Amelia Bedelia got the apples. She called
some children. "There is a problem for each
of you," she said. "You all have apples.
Somebody is going to try to take some away.
Are you going to let them?"

"No!" shouted the children.

Amelia Bedelia went to the other children.
"You are supposed to take away some of their
apples," she said. She told each child whom
to take from. "Can you do that?" she said.

"Sure!" said the children.

"All right, everybody," said Amelia
Bedelia. "Go!"

Children started after each other. They
ran all over the yard.

Amelia Bedelia turned and went into the

kitchen. She put some of this and a lot of that into a big pot. She put the pot on the stove. "There," she said. "I'll surprise them."

Amelia Bedelia started out. Just then Mr. Rogers started in.

"What is all of this?" said Mr. Rogers. "What are those children doing?"

"Math," said Amelia Bedelia.

"Math!" said Mr. Rogers.

"Come see," said Amelia Bedelia.

They went out.

"That's not fair, Steve," yelled Janet. "You hid your apples. I can't take any."

"That's not fair, Judy," shouted Andy. "You took away all my apples."

"What in tarnation are they doing?" said Mr. Rogers.

Amelia Bedelia read him the problems.

"That sounds like fun. I'm going to help them," he said. He joined the children.

"Now that does beat all," said Amelia Bedelia.

She went inside. Later she called, "Everybody come. All apples on the table."

Apples came from everywhere. Amelia Bedelia put a stick in each one. Then she dipped them in the pot.

"Taffy apples!" everybody shouted.

"Right," said Amelia Bedelia. "Take one
and go home. School is out."

The children grabbed apples. They
crowded around Amelia Bedelia.

"Please, please teach us again," each one said.

Amelia Bedelia said nothing. She looked at her kitchen and shook her head.

Mrs. Rogers walked in. Someone was with her.

"What happened?" she said, "Where are the children?"

"Home," said Amelia Bedelia.

"Home!" said Mrs. Rogers. "But it's not time."

"It was for me," said Amelia Bedelia.

"This is Miss Reed," said Mrs. Rogers. "She is the new teacher. She came to get the children."

"Then she will have to find them," said Amelia Bedelia. "I'm plumb tired out."

"But, but . . ." said Miss Reed.

"More taffy apples," called Mr. Rogers.

"Taffy apples!" said Mrs. Rogers. "Come on, Miss Reed."

Amelia Bedelia put the taffy apples on the table. They all sat down and ate.

"I'll let you teach anytime," said Miss Reed, "if you will make taffy apples."

"Be glad to," said Amelia Bedelia. "I do love children."

❧

Whatever else, Amelia Bedelia is certainly different—and funny. Peggy Parish has written a number of Amelia Bedelia books. You might try *Play Ball, Amelia Bedelia*, in which Amelia Bedelia makes a mess of a baseball game. Or, watch her create confusion in the Rogers' household in *Good Work, Amelia Bedelia*.

The Fox Went Out
on a Chilly Night

an old folk song

The fox went out on a chilly night,
And begged the moon to give him light,
For he had many a mile to go that night
Before he reached the town-o!
    Town-o! town-o!
For he had many a mile to go that night
Before he reached the town-o!

Well he ran 'til he came to a great big pen,
Where the ducks and the geese were kept therein.
"A couple of you gonna grease my chin
Before I leave this town-o!
　　Town-o! town-o!
A couple of you gonna grease my chin
Before I leave this town-o!"

He grabbed the gray goose by the neck,
And flung a duck across his back;
He did not mind the "Quack! quack! quack!"
And their legs all dangling down-o!
    Down-o! down-o!
He did not mind the "Quack! quack! quack!"
And their legs all dangling down-o!

Old Mother Flipper Flapper jumped out of bed,
Out of the window she popped her head,
Crying, "John, John, the gray goose is gone
And the fox is on the town-o!
    Town-o! town-o!"
Crying, "John, John, the gray goose is gone
And the fox is on the town-o!"

The fox he ran 'til he came to his den,
And there were his little ones, eight, nine, ten,
Crying, "Daddy, Daddy, better go back again,
'Cause it must be a mighty fine town-o!
　　Town-o! town-o!"
Crying, "Daddy, Daddy, better go back again,
'Cause it must be a mighty fine town-o!"

Then the fox and his wife, without any strife,
Cut up the goose with a carving knife.
They never had such a supper in their life,
And the little ones chewed on the bones-o!
    Bones-o! bones-o!
They never had such a supper in their life,
And the little ones chewed on the bones-o!

The Family Dog

from *Tales of a Fourth Grade Nothing*
by Judy Blume

I won Dribble at Jimmy Fargo's birthday
party. All the other guys got to take home
goldfish in little plastic bags. I won him
because I guessed there were three hundred
and forty-eight jellybeans in Mrs. Fargo's jar.
Really, there were four hundred and
twenty-three, she told us later. Still, my
guess was closest. "Peter Warren Hatcher is
the big winner!" Mrs. Fargo announced.

At first I felt bad that I didn't get a goldfish too. Then Jimmy handed me a glass bowl. Inside there was some water and three rocks. A tiny green turtle was sleeping on the biggest rock. All the other guys looked at their goldfish. I knew what they were thinking. They wished they could have tiny green turtles too.

I named my turtle Dribble while I was walking home from Jimmy's party. I live at 25 West 68th Street. It's an old apartment building. But it's got one of the best elevators in New York City. There are mirrors all around. You can see yourself from every angle. There's a soft, cushioned bench to sit on if you're too tired to stand. The elevator operator's name is Henry Bevelheimer. He lets us call him Henry because Bevelheimer's very hard to say.

Our apartment's on the twelfth floor. But I don't have to tell Henry. He already knows. He knows everybody in the building. He's that smart! He even knows I'm nine and in fourth grade.

I showed him Dribble right away. "I won him at a birthday party," I said.

Henry smiled. "Your mother's going to be surprised."

Henry was right. My mother was really

surprised. Her mouth opened when I said,
"Just look at what I won at Jimmy Fargo's
birthday party." I held up my tiny green
turtle. "I've already named him ... Dribble!
Isn't that a great name for a turtle?"

My mother made a face. "I don't like the
way he smells," she said.

"What do you mean?" I asked. I put my
nose right down close to him. I didn't smell
anything but turtle. *So Dribble smells like
turtle*, I thought. *Well, he's supposed to.
That's what he is!*

"And I'm not going to take care of him
either," my mother added.

"Of course you're not," I told her. "He's my turtle. And I'm the one who's going to take care of him."

"You're going to change his water and clean out his bowl and feed him and all of that?" she asked.

"Yes," I said. "And even more. I'm going to see to it that he's happy!"

This time my mother made a funny noise. Like a groan.

I went into my bedroom. I put Dribble on top of my dresser. I tried to pet him and tell him he would be happy living with me. But it isn't easy to pet a turtle. They aren't soft and furry and they don't lick you or anything. Still, I had my very own pet at last.

Later, when I sat down at the dinner table, my mother said, "I smell turtle. Peter, go and *scrub* your hands!"

Some people might think that my mother is my biggest problem. She doesn't like turtles and she's always telling me to scrub my hands. That doesn't mean just run them under the water. *Scrub* means I'm supposed to use soap and rub my hands together. Then I've got to rinse and dry them. I ought to know by now. I've heard it enough!

But my mother isn't my biggest problem. Neither is my father. He spends a lot of time watching commercials on TV. That's because he's in the advertising business. These days his favorite commercial is the one about Juicy-O. He wrote it himself. And the president of the Juicy-O company liked it so much he sent my father a whole crate of Juicy-O for our family to drink. It tastes like a combination of oranges, pineapples, grapefruits, pears, and bananas. (And if you want to know the truth, I'm getting pretty sick of drinking it.) But Juicy-O isn't my biggest problem either.

My biggest problem is my brother, Farley Drexel Hatcher. He's two-and-a-half years old. Everybody calls him Fudge. I feel sorry for him if he's going to grow up with a name like Fudge, but I don't say a word. It's none of my business.

Fudge is always in my way. He messes up everything he sees. And when he gets mad he throws himself flat on the floor and he screams. *And* he kicks. *And* he bangs his fists. The only time I really like him is when he's sleeping. He sucks four fingers on his left hand and makes a slurping noise.

When Fudge saw Dribble he said, "Ohhhhh . . . see!"

And I said, "That's *my* turtle, get it? *Mine!* You don't touch him."

Fudge said, "No touch." Then he laughed like crazy.

Nobody ever came right out and said that Fudge was the reason my father lost the Juicy-O account. But I thought about it. My father said he was glad. Now he could spend more time on his other clients—like the Toddle-Bike Company. My father is in charge of their new TV commercial.

I thought maybe he could use me in it since I know how to stand on my head. But he said he wasn't planning on having any head-standers in the commercial.

I learned to stand on my head in gym

class. I'm pretty good at it too. I can stay up
for as long as three minutes. I showed my
mother, my father, and Fudge how I can do
it right in the living room. They were all
impressed. Especially Fudge. He wanted to
do it too. So I turned him upside down and
tried to teach him. But he always tumbled
over backwards.

Right after I learned to stand on my
head Fudge stopped eating. He did it
suddenly. One day he ate fine and the next
day nothing. "No eat!" he told my mother.

She didn't pay too much attention to him
until the third day. When he still refused to

eat she got upset. "You've got to eat, Fudgie," she said. "You want to grow up to be big and strong, don't you?"

"No grow!" Fudge said.

That night my mother told my father how worried she was about Fudge. So my father did tricks for him while my mother stood over his chair trying to get some food into his mouth. But nothing worked. Not even juggling oranges.

Finally my mother got the brilliant idea of me standing on my head while she fed Fudge. I wasn't very excited about standing on my head in the kitchen. The floor was awfully hard in there. But my mother begged me. She said, "It's very important for Fudge to eat. Please help us, Peter."

So I stood on my head. When Fudge saw me upside down he clapped his hands and laughed. When he laughs he opens his mouth. That's when my mother stuffed some baked potato into it.

But the next morning I put my foot down. "No! I don't want to stand on my head in the kitchen. Or anywhere else!" I added, "And if I don't hurry I'll be late for school."

"Don't you care if your brother starves?"

"No!" I told her.

"Peter! What an awful thing to say."

"Oh . . . he'll eat when he gets hungry. Why don't you just leave him alone!"

That afternoon when I came home from school I found my brother on the kitchen floor playing with boxes of cereals and raisins and dried apricots. My mother was begging him to eat.

"No, no, no!" Fudge shouted. He made a terrible mess, dumping everything on the floor.

"Please stand on your head, Peter," my mother said. "It's the only way he'll eat."

"No!" I told her. "I'm not going to stand on my head anymore." I went into my room and slammed the door. I played with Dribble until suppertime. Nobody ever worries about me the way they worry about Fudge. If I decided not to eat they'd probably never even notice!

That night during dinner Fudge hid under the kitchen table. He said, "I'm a doggie. Woof . . . woof . . . woof!"

It was hard to eat with him under the table pulling on my legs. I waited for my father to say something. But he didn't.

Finally my mother jumped up. "I know," she said. "If Fudgie's a doggie he wants to eat on the floor! Right?"

If you ask me Fudge never even thought about that. But he liked the idea a lot. He barked and nodded his head. So my mother fixed his plate and put it under the table. Then she reached down and petted him, like he was a real dog.

My father said, "Aren't we carrying this a little too far?"

My mother didn't answer.

Fudge ate two bites of his dinner.

My mother was satisfied.

After a week of having him eat under the table I felt like we really did have a family dog. I thought how great it would be if we could trade Fudge for a nice cocker spaniel. That would solve all my problems. I'd

walk him and feed him and play with him.
He could even sleep on the edge of my bed at
night. But of course that was wishful
thinking. My brother is here to stay. And
there's nothing much I can do about it.

Grandma came over with a million ideas
about getting Fudge to eat. She tricked him
by making milk shakes in the blender. When
Fudge wasn't looking she threw in an egg.
Then she told him if he drank it all up there
would be a surprise in the bottom of the
glass. The first time he believed her. He
finished his milk shake. But all he saw was
an empty glass. There wasn't any surprise!
Fudge got so mad he threw the glass down.
It smashed into little pieces. After that
Grandma left.

The next day my mother dragged Fudge to

Dr. Cone's office. He told her to leave him alone. That Fudge would eat when he got hungry.

I reminded my mother that I'd told her the same thing—and for free! But I guess my mother didn't believe either one of us because she took Fudge to see three more doctors. None of them could find a thing wrong with my brother. One doctor even suggested that my mother cook Fudge his favorite foods.

So that night my mother broiled lamb chops just for Fudge. The rest of us ate stew. She served him the two little lamb chops on his plate under the table. Just the smell of them was enough to make my stomach growl. I thought it was mean of my mother to make them for Fudge and not for me.

Fudge looked at his lamb chops for a few minutes. Then he pushed his plate away. "No!" he said. "No chops!"

"Fudgie . . . you'll starve!" my mother cried. "You *must* eat!"

"No chops! Corn Flakes," Fudge said. "Want Corn Flakes!"

My mother ran to get the cereal for Fudge. "You can eat the chops if you want them, Peter," she told me.

I reached down and helped myself to the lamb chops. My mother handed Fudge his bowl of cereal. But he didn't eat it. He sat at my feet and looked up at me. He watched me eat his chops.

"Eat your cereal!" my father said.

"NO! NO EAT CEREAL!" Fudge yelled.

My father was really mad. His face turned bright red. He said, "Fudge, you will eat that cereal or you will wear it!"

This was turning out to be fun after all, I thought. And the lamb chops were really tasty. I dipped the bone in some Ketchup and chewed away.

Fudge messed around with his cereal for a minute. Then he looked at my father and said, "NO EAT . . . NO EAT . . . NO EAT!"

My father wiped his mouth with his napkin, pushed back his chair, and got up

from the table. He picked up the bowl of
cereal in one hand, and Fudge in the other.
He carried them both into the bathroom. I
went along, nibbling on a bone, to see what
was going to happen.

My father stood Fudge in the tub and
dumped the whole bowl of cereal right over
his head. Fudge screamed. He sure can
scream loud.

My father motioned for me to go back to
the kitchen. He joined us in a minute. We sat

down and finished our dinner. Fudge kept on screaming. My mother wanted to go to him but my father told her to stay where she was. He'd had enough of Fudge's monkey business at mealtimes.

I think my mother really was relieved that my father had taken over. For once my brother got what he deserved. And I was glad!

The next day Fudge sat at the table again. In his little red booster chair, where he belongs. He ate everything my mother put in front of him. "No more doggie," he told us.

And for a long time after that his favorite expression was "eat it or wear it!"

⚜

Peter finds Fudge harder and harder to take—as you will discover by reading the rest of *Tales of a Fourth Grade Nothing*, as well as the sequel, *Superfudge*. And if you still want a good laugh, try another of Judy Blume's books, *Freckle Juice*.

Alligator Pie
by Dennis Lee

Alligator pie, alligator pie,
If I don't get some I think I'm gonna die.
Give away the green grass, give away the sky,
But don't give away my alligator pie.

Alligator stew, alligator stew,
If I don't get some I don't know what I'll do.
Give away my furry hat, give away my shoe,
But don't give away my alligator stew.

Alligator soup, alligator soup,
If I don't get some I think I'm gonna droop.
Give away my hockey-stick, give away my hoop,
But don't give away my alligator soup.

I Met a Man
author unknown

As I was going up the stair
I met a man who wasn't there.
He wasn't there again today—
Oh! how I wish he'd go away!

Pie Problem
by Shel Silverstein

If I eat one more piece of pie, I'll die!
If I can't have one more piece of pie, I'll die!
So since it's all decided I must die,
I might as well have one more piece of pie.
MMMM—OOOH—MY!
Chomp—Gulp—'Bye.

The Dragon of Grindly Grun

by Shel Silverstein

I'm the Dragon of Grindly Grun,
I breathe fire as hot as the sun.
When a knight comes to fight
I just toast him on sight,
Like a hot crispy cinnamon bun.

When I see a fair damsel go by,
I just sigh a fiery sigh,
And she's baked like a 'tater—
I think of her later
With a romantic tear in my eye.

I'm the Dragon of Grindly Grun,
But my lunches aren't very much fun,
For I like my damsels medium rare,
And they *always* come out well done.

Eat-it-all Elaine

by Kaye Starbird

I went away last August
To summer camp in Maine,
And there I met a camper
Called Eat-it-all Elaine.
Although Elaine was quiet,
She liked to cause a stir
By acting out the nickname
Her camp-mates gave to her.

The day of our arrival
At Cabin Number Three
When girls kept coming over
To greet Elaine and me,
She took a piece of Kleenex
And calmly chewed it up,
Then strolled outside the cabin
And ate a buttercup.

Elaine, from that day forward,
Was always in command.
On hikes, she'd eat some birch-bark.
On swims, she'd eat some sand.
At meals, she'd swallow prune-pits
And never have a pain,
While everyone around her
Would giggle, "Oh, Elaine!"

One morning, berry-picking,
A bug was in her pail,
And though we thought for certain
Her appetite would fail,
Elaine said, "Hmm, a stinkbug."
And while we murmured, "Ooh,"
She ate her pail of berries
And ate the stinkbug, too.

The night of Final Banquet
When counselors were handing
Awards to different children
Whom they believed outstanding,
To every *thinking* person
At summer camp in Maine
The Most Outstanding Camper
Was Eat-it-all Elaine.

Table Manners

by Gelett Burgess

The Goops they lick their fingers,
    And the Goops they lick their knives;
They spill their broth on the tablecloth—
    Oh, they lead disgusting lives!
The Goops they talk while eating,
    And loud and fast they chew;
And that is why I'm glad that I
    Am not a Goop—are you?

Little Bits of Soft-Boiled Egg

by Fay Maschler

Little bits of soft-boiled egg
Spread along the table leg
Annoy a parent even more
Than toast and jam dropped on the floor.
(When you're bashing on the ketchup
Keep in mind where it might fetch up.)
Try to keep the food you eat
Off your clothes and off your seat,
On your plate and fork and knife.
This holds true throughout your life.

The Alligator
by Mary Macdonald

The alligator chased his tail
Which hit him on the snout;
He nibbled, gobbled, swallowed it,
And turned right inside-out.

My Little Sister
by William Wise

My little sister
Likes to eat.
But when she does
She's not too neat.
The trouble is
She doesn't know
Exactly where
The food should go!

I Eat My Peas with Honey
author unknown

I eat my peas with honey;
I've done it all my life.
It makes the peas taste funny,
But it keeps them on the knife.

The Vulture
by Hilaire Belloc

The Vulture eats between his meals,
　　And that's the reason why
He very, very rarely feels
　　As well as you and I.

His eye is dull, his head is bald,
　　His neck is growing thinner.
Oh! what a lesson for us all
　　To only eat at dinner!

143

A Thousand Pails of Water

by Ronald Roy

Yukio lived in a village where people fished and hunted whales to make their living. Yukio's father, too, was a whale hunter.

"Why do you kill the whales, Father?" Yukio asked. "Suki's father works in the market and his hands are never red from blood."

"Hunting the whale is all I know," his father answered.

But Yukio did not understand.

Yukio went to his grandfather and asked again. "Why does my father kill the whales?"

"Your father does what he must do," his grandfather said. "Let him be, little one, and ask your questions of the sea."

So Yukio went to the sea.

Small creatures scurried from under his feet in the tide pools. Large scavenger birds screamed at him from the sky, "Bring us food!"

Then Yukio saw a whale that had become lodged between some rocks and was left behind when the tide went out.

The large tail flukes beat the sand, helplessly. The eye, as big as Yukio's hand, rolled in fright.

Yukio knew that the whale would not live long out of the sea.

"I will help you, sir," he said.

But how? The whale was huge, like a temple.

Yukio raced to the water's edge. Was the tide coming in or going out? In, he decided, by the way the little fingers of foam climbed higher with each new wave.

The sun was hot on Yukio's back as he stood looking at the whale.

Yukio filled his pail with water and threw it over the great head.

"You are so big and my pail is so small!" he cried. "But I will throw a thousand pails of water over you before I stop."

The second pail went on the head as well, and the third and the fourth. But Yukio knew he must wet every part of the whale or it would die in the sun.

Yukio made many trips to the sea for water, counting as he went. He threw four pails on the body, then four on the tail, and then three on the head.

There was a little shade on one side of the big gray prisoner. Yukio sat there, out of breath, his heart pounding. Then he looked in the whale's eye and remembered his promise.

Yukio went back to the sea and stooped
to fill his pail. How many had he filled so
far? He had lost count. But he knew he must
not stop.

Yukio fell, the precious water spilling
from his pail. He cried, and his tears
disappeared into the sand.

A wave touched his foot, as if to say,
"Get up and carry more water. I am coming,
but I am very slow."

Yukio filled his pail over and over. His
back hurt, and his arms—but he threw and
threw.

He fell again, but this time he did not get up.

Yukio felt himself being lifted.

"You have worked hard, little one. Now let us help."

Yukio's grandfather lay him in the shade of one of the rocks. Yukio watched his grandfather throw his first pail of water and go for another.

"Hurry!" Yukio wanted to scream, for his grandfather was old and walked slowly.

Then Yukio heard the voices. His father and the village people were running toward the sea. They carried pails and buckets and anything that would hold water.

Some of the villagers removed their jackets and soaked them in the sea. These they placed on the whale's burning skin. Soon the whale was wet all over.

Slowly the sea came closer and closer. At last it covered the huge tail. The village people ran back and forth carrying water, shouting to each other. Yukio knew the whale would be saved.

Yukio's father came and stood by him. "Thank you, Father," Yukio said, "for bringing the village people to help."

"You are strong and good," his father said, "But to save a whale many hands must carry the water."

Now the whale was moving with each new wave. Suddenly a great one lifted him free of the rocks. He was still for a moment, then, with a flip of his tail, swam out to sea.

The villagers watched silently, as the whale swam farther and farther from their shore. Then they turned and walked toward the village.

Except for Yukio, who was asleep in the arms of his father.

He had carried a thousand pails of water, and he was tired.

You will find many other stories about life in Japan in your school or public library. Here are three that you should enjoy: *Story of the Grateful Crane* retold by Jennifer Bartoli; *Momotaro the Peach Boy* edited by Ruth Tabrah; and *The One-legged Ghost* by Betty Jean Lifton.

The Eensy, Weensy Spider
author unknown

The eensy, weensy spider
Climbed up the waterspout.
Down came the rain
And washed the spider out.
Out came the sun
And dried up all the rain.
So the eensy, weensy spider
Climbed up the spout again.

In summer the rains come,
The grass grows up,
and the deer has new horns.
a Yaqui Indian song

Rain
by Robert Louis Stevenson

The rain is raining all around,
It falls on field and tree,
It rains on the umbrellas here,
And on the ships at sea.

Spring Rain
by Marchette Chute

The storm came up so very quick
    It couldn't have been quicker.
I should have brought my hat along,
    I should have brought my slicker.

My hair is wet, my feet are wet,
    I couldn't be much wetter.
I fell into a river once
    But this is even better.

Until I Saw the Sea
by Lilian Moore

Until I saw the sea
I did not know
that wind
could wrinkle water so.

I never knew
that sun
could splinter a whole sea of blue.

Nor
did I know before,
a sea breathes in and out
upon a shore.

The Sea
author unknown

Behold the wonders of the mighty deep,
Where crabs and lobsters learn to creep,
And little fishes learn to swim,
And clumsy sailors tumble in.

Sea Gull
by Elizabeth Coatsworth

The sea gull curves his wings,
the sea gull turns his eyes.
Get down into the water, fish!
(if you are wise.)

The sea gull slants his wings,
the sea gull turns his head.
Get deep into the water, fish!
(or you'll be dead.)

Hurt No Living Thing
by Christina Rossetti

Hurt no living thing;
Ladybird, nor butterfly,
Nor moth with dusty wing,
Nor cricket chirping cheerily,
Nor grasshopper so light of leap,
Nor dancing gnat, nor beetle fat,
Nor harmless worms that creep.

Because I am poor,
I pray for every living creature.

a Kiowa Indian song

Onto a boy's arm came a mosquito.
"Don't hit! Don't hit!" it hummed,
"Grandchildren have I to sing to."
"Imagine," the boy said,
"So small and yet a grandfather."

an Eastern Eskimo song

The Frog
by Hilaire Belloc

Be kind and tender to the Frog,
  And do not call him names,
As "Slimy skin," or "Polly-wog,"
  Or likewise "Ugly James,"
Or "Gape-a-grin," or "Toad-gone-wrong,"
  Or "Billy Bandy-knees":
The Frog is justly sensitive
  To epithets like these.
No animal will more repay
  A treatment kind and fair;
At least so lonely people say
Who keep a frog (and, by the way,
  They are extremely rare).

Sam, Bangs & Moonshine

by Evaline Ness

On a small island, near a large harbor, there once lived a fisherman's little daughter (named Samantha, but always called Sam), who had the reckless habit of lying.

Not even the sailors home from the sea could tell stranger stories than Sam. Not even the ships in the harbor, with curious cargoes from giraffes to gerbils, claimed more wonders than Sam did.

Sam said her mother was a mermaid, when everyone knew she was dead.

Sam said she had a fierce lion at home, and a baby kangaroo. (Actually, what she *really* had was an old wise cat called Bangs.)

Sam even said that Bangs could talk if and when he wanted to.

Sam said this. Sam said that. But whatever Sam said you could never believe.

Even Bangs yawned and shook his head when she said the ragged old rug on the doorstep was a chariot drawn by dragons.

Early one morning, before Sam's father left in his fishing boat to be gone all day, he hugged Sam hard and said, "Today, for a change, talk REAL not MOONSHINE. MOONSHINE spells trouble."

Sam promised. But while she washed the dishes, made the beds, and swept the floor, she wondered what he meant. When she

asked Bangs to explain REAL and
MOONSHINE, Bangs jumped on her shoulder
and purred, "MOONSHINE is flummadiddle.
REAL is the opposite."

Sam decided that Bangs made no sense
whatever.

When the sun made a golden star on the
cracked window, Sam knew it was time to
expect Thomas.

Thomas lived in the tall grand house on
the hill. Thomas had two cows in the barn,
twenty-five sheep, a bicycle with a basket,
and a jungle-gym on the lawn. But most

important of all, Thomas believed every word Sam said.

At the same time every day Thomas rode his bicycle down the hill to Sam's house and begged to see her baby kangaroo.

Every day Sam told Thomas it had just "stepped out." She sent Thomas everywhere to find it. She sent him to the tallest trees where, she said, it was visiting owls. Or perhaps it was up in the old windmill, grinding corn for its evening meal.

"It might be," said Sam, "in the lighthouse tower, warning ships at sea."

"Or maybe," she said, "it's asleep on the sand. Somewhere, anywhere on the beach."

Wherever Sam sent Thomas, he went. He climbed up trees, ran down steps, and scoured the beach, but he never found Sam's baby kangaroo.

While Thomas searched, Sam sat in her chariot and was drawn by dragons to faraway secret worlds.

Today, when Thomas arrived, Sam said, "That baby kangaroo just left to visit my mermaid mother. She lives in a cave behind Blue Rock."

Sam watched Thomas race away on his bicycle over the narrow strand that stretched to a massive blue rock in the distance. Then she sat down in her chariot. Bangs came out of the house and sat down beside Sam. With his head turned in the direction of the diminishing Thomas, Bangs said, "When the tide comes up, it covers the road to Blue Rock. Tide rises early today."

Sam looked at Bangs for a minute. Then she said, "Pardon me while I go to the moon."

Bangs stood up. He stretched his front legs. Then he stretched his back legs. Slowly he stalked away from Sam toward Blue Rock.

Suddenly Sam had no desire to go to the moon. Or any other place either. She just sat in her chariot and thought about Bangs and Thomas.

She was so busy thinking that she was unaware of thick muddy clouds that blocked out the sun. Nor did she hear the menacing rumble of thunder. She was almost knocked off the doorstep when a sudden gust of wind drove torrents of rain against her face.

Sam leaped into the house and slammed the door. She went to the window to look at Blue Rock, but she could see nothing through the grey ribbed curtain of rain. She wondered where Thomas was. She wondered where Bangs was. Sam stood there looking at nothing, trying to swallow the lump that rose in her throat.

The murky light in the room deepened to black. Sam was still at the window when her father burst into the house. Water streamed

from his hat and oozed from his boots. Sam ran
to him screaming, "Bangs and Thomas are out
on the rock! Blue Rock! Bangs and Thomas!"

As her father turned quickly and ran out
the door, he ordered Sam to stay in the house.

"And pray that the tide hasn't covered
the rock!" he yelled.

When her father had gone, Sam sat down.
She listened to the rain hammer on the tin
roof. Then suddenly it stopped. Sam closed her
eyes and mouth, tight. She waited in the quiet
room. It seemed to her that she waited forever.

At last she heard her father's footsteps outside. She flung open the door and said one word: "Bangs?"

Sam's father shook his head.

"He was washed away," he said. "But I found Thomas on the rock. I brought him back in the boat. He's home now, safe in bed. Can you tell me how all this happened?"

Sam started to explain, but sobs choked her. She cried so hard that it was a long time before her father understood everything.

Finally, Sam's father said, "Go to bed now. But before you go to sleep, Sam, tell yourself the difference between REAL and MOONSHINE."

Sam went to her room and crept into
bed. With her eyes wide open she thought
about REAL and MOONSHINE.

MOONSHINE was a mermaid-mother, a
fierce lion, a chariot drawn by dragons, and
certainly a baby kangaroo. It was all
flummadiddle just as Bangs had told her. Or
had he told her? Wouldn't her father say that
a cat's talking was MOONSHINE?

REAL was no mother at all. REAL was
her father and Bangs. And now there wasn't
even Bangs. Tears welled up in Sam's eyes
again. They ran down into her ears making a
scratching noise. Sam sat up and blew her
nose. The scratching was not in her ears. It

was at the window. As Sam stared at the black oblong, two enormous yellow eyes appeared and stared back. Sam sprang from her bed and opened the window. There sat Bangs, his coat a sodden mess.

"Oh Bangs!" cried Sam, as she grabbed and smothered him with kisses. "What happened to you?"

In a few words Bangs told her that one moment he was on the rock with Thomas and the next he was lying at the foot of the lighthouse tower a mile away. All done by waves.

"Nasty stuff, water," Bangs grumbled, as he washed himself from his ears to his feet.

Sam patted Bangs. "Well, at least it's not flummadiddle. . . ." Sam paused. She looked up to see her father standing in the doorway.

"Look! Bangs is home!" shouted Sam.

"Hello, Bangs. What's not flummadiddle?" asked Sam's father.

"Bangs! And you! And Thomas!" answered Sam. "Oh, Daddy! I'll always know the difference between REAL and MOONSHINE now. Bangs and Thomas were almost lost because of MOONSHINE Bangs told me."

"He *told* you?" questioned Sam's father.

"Well, he would have *if* he could talk," said Sam. Then she added sadly, "I know cats can't talk like people, but I almost believed I *did* have a baby kangaroo."

Her father looked steadily at her.

"There's good MOONSHINE and bad MOONSHINE," he said. "The important thing is to know the difference." He kissed Sam good night and left the room.

When he had closed the door, Sam said, "You know, Bangs, I might just keep my chariot."

This time Bangs did not yawn and shake his head. Instead he licked her hand. He waited until she got into bed, then he curled up at her feet and went to sleep.

The next morning Sam opened her eyes
to see an incredible thing! Hopping toward
her on its hind legs was a small, elegant, large-
eyed animal with a long tail like a lion's.
Behind it strolled Bangs and her father.

"A baby kangaroo!" shouted Sam.
"Where did you find it!"

"It is *not* a baby kangaroo," said Sam's
father. "It's a gerbil. I found it on an African
banana boat in the harbor."

"Now Thomas can see a baby kangaroo
at last!" Sam squealed with joy.

Sam's father interrupted her. "Stop the
MOONSHINE, Sam. Call it by its REAL name.
Anyway, Thomas won't come today. He's
sick in bed with laryngitis. He can't even
talk. Also his bicycle got lost in the storm."

Sam looked down at the gerbil. Gently
she stroked its tiny head. Without raising her
eyes, she said, "Daddy, do you think I should
give the gerbil to Thomas?"

Sam's father said nothing. Bangs licked
his tail.

Suddenly Sam hollered, "Come on, Bangs!"

She jumped out of bed and slipped into
her shoes. As she grabbed her coat, she picked
up the gerbil, and ran from the house with
Bangs at her heels. Sam did not stop running
until she stood at the side of Thomas' bed.

Very carefully she placed the gerbil on Thomas' stomach. The little animal sat straight up on its long hind legs and gazed directly at Thomas with its immense round eyes.

"Whaaaaaaaaaa sis name!" wheezed Thomas.

"MOONSHINE," answered Sam, as she gave Bangs a big wide smile.

⚜

Evaline Ness has written and illustrated many books. One you might like is *Do You Have the Time, Lydia?* It is about a girl who is involved in so many projects she can never finish anything she starts. And if you have ever had a day when nothing went right, you will enjoy *Alexander and the Terrible, Horrible, No Good, Very Bad Day* by Judith Viorst.

Bedtime

by Eleanor Farjeon

Five minutes, five minutes more, please!
   Let me stay five minutes more!
Can't I just finish the castle
   I'm building here on the floor?
Can't I just finish the story
   I'm reading here in my book?
Can't I just finish this bead-chain—
   It *almost* is finished, look!
Can't I just finish this game, please?
   When a game's once begun
It's a pity never to find out
   Whether you've lost or won.
Can't I just stay five minutes?
   Well, can't I stay just four?
Three minutes, then? two minutes?
   Can't I stay *one* minute more?

Rules

by Karla Kuskin

Do not jump on ancient uncles.
      *

Do not yell at average mice.
      *

Do not wear a broom to breakfast.
      *

Do not ask a snake's advice.
      *

Do not bathe in chocolate pudding.
      *

Do not talk to bearded bears.
      *

Do not smoke cigars on sofas.
      *

Do not dance on velvet chairs.
      *

Do not take a whale to visit
Russell's mother's cousin's yacht.
      *

And whatever else you do do
It is better you
Do not.

Bedtime Stories

by Lilian Moore

"Tell me a story,"
Says Witch's Child.

"About the Beast
So fierce and wild.

About a Ghost
That shrieks and groans.

A Skeleton
That rattles bones.

About a Monster
Crawly-creepy.

Something nice
To make me sleepy."

My Dragon
by X. J. Kennedy

I have a purple dragon
With a long brass tail that clangs,
And anyone not nice to me
Soon feels his fiery fangs,

So if you tell me I'm a dope
Or call my muscles jelly,
You just might dwell a billion years
Inside his boiling belly.

The Gold-Tinted Dragon
by Karla Kuskin

What's the good of a wagon
Without any dragon
To pull you for mile after mile?
An elegant lean one
A gold-tinted green one
Wearing a dragonly smile.
You'll sweep down the valleys
You'll sail up the hills
Your dragon will shine in the sun
And as you rush by
The people will cry
"I wish that my wagon had one!"

The Toaster
by William Jay Smith

A silver-scaled Dragon with jaws flaming red
Sits at my elbow and toasts my bread.
I hand him fat slices, and then, one by one,
He hands them back when he sees they are done.

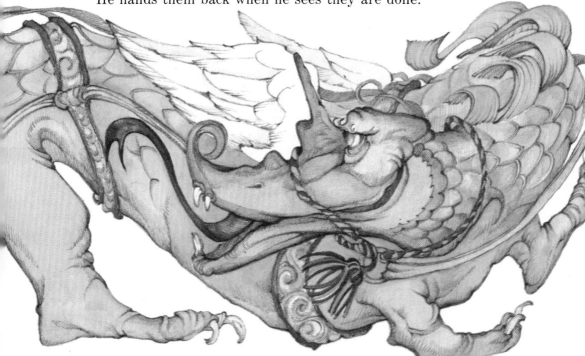

The Moon's the North Wind's Cooky
by Vachel Lindsay

The Moon's the North Wind's cooky,
He bites it day by day,
Until there's but a rim of scraps
That crumble all away.

The South Wind is a baker.
He kneads clouds in his den,
And bakes a crisp new moon *that . . . greedy*
North . . . Wind . . . eats . . . again!

Encyclopedia Brown

from *Encyclopedia Brown, Boy Detective*
by Donald J. Sobol

Leroy Brown's head is full of facts, which is why he is
called Encyclopedia. Because he often helps his father,
the Chief of Police in Idaville, solve cases, he set up
his own detective agency. Here is your chance to
match wits with Encyclopedia. In the two cases that
follow, all the clues are there for you to find. Can *you*
solve the mystery?

✤ ✤ ✤

The Case of Merko's Grandson

Bugs Meany and his Tigers liked to spend
rainy afternoons in their clubhouse. Usually,
they sat around thinking up ways of getting
even with Encyclopedia Brown.

But today they had met for another
purpose—to cheer the boy detective on.

Encyclopedia and Sally Kimball were
about to meet in a battle of brains.

The Tigers hated Sally even more than
they hated Encyclopedia—and with good reason.

When Sally had moved into the

neighborhood two months ago, the Tigers jumped to show off for her. She was very pretty and she was very good at sports.

In fact, she got up a team of fifth-grade girls and challenged the Tigers to a game of softball. The boys thought it was a big joke, till Sally started striking them out. She was the whole team. In the last inning she hit the home run that won for the girls, 1-0.

But the real blow fell on the Tigers the next day.

Bugs was bullying a small boy when Sally happened to ride by on her bicycle.

"Let him go!" she ordered, hopping to the ground.

Bugs snarled. The snarl changed to a gasp as Sally broke his grip on the boy.

Before the other Tigers knew what to do, Sally had knocked their leader down with a quick left to the jaw.

Bugs bounced up, surprised and angry. He pushed Sally. She hit him again, with a right to the jaw. Bugs said *oooh*, and went down again.

For the next thirty seconds Bugs bounced up and down like a beach ball. By the fourth bounce, he was getting up a lot more slowly than he was going down.

"I'm going to make you sorry," he said.

But his voice was weak, and he wore the sick
smile of a boy who had taken one ride too
many on a roller coaster.

"So?" said Sally. She moved her feet and
took careful aim.

"This," she said, aiming another blow,
"should take the frosting off you."

Bugs landed on his back, flat as a
fifteen-cent sandwich. Not until Sally had
ridden away did he dare get up.

Sally was not content to rest on her
victories at softball and fighting. She aimed
higher.

She set out to prove she was not only

stronger than any boy up to twelve years of age in Idaville, but smarter, too!

That meant out-thinking the thinking machine, Encyclopedia Brown.

The great battle of brains took place in the Tigers' clubhouse. The two champions, seated on orange crates, faced each other. The Tigers crowded behind Encyclopedia. The girls' softball team crowded behind Sally. That left just enough room in the tool shed to think.

Everyone stopped talking when Peter Clinton, the referee, announced the rules.

"Sally has five minutes to tell a mystery. She must give all the clues. Then Encyclopedia will have five minutes to solve the mystery. Ready, you two?"

"Ready," said the girl champion.

"Ready," said Encyclopedia, closing his eyes.

"Go!" called Peter, eyes on his watch.

Sally began to tell the story:

"The Great Merko was the best trapeze artist the world had ever seen. People in every big city were thrilled by the wonderful performer swinging fifty feet above the ground!

"In the year 1922, Merko died at the very height of fame. In Merko's desk was found a letter. It was a will, written by the circus star. The will directed that the star's money be put in a bank for forty years.

"After forty years, the money was to be taken out and given to Merko's oldest grandson. If no grandson was alive, all the money was to go to Merko's nearest relative, man or woman.

"Forty years passed. A search was begun. At last a man was found in Kansas City who said he was Merko's grandson. His name was Fred Gibson. He went to court to claim his inheritance.

"While the judge was listening to him, a

tall woman in the back of the courtroom
jumped up. She was very excited.

"The woman said she was the trapeze
artist's grandniece. She kept shouting that
the Great Merko was not Fred Gibson's
grandfather. Therefore, the money was
rightfully hers.

"The judge questioned the woman. He
had to agree with what she said. She was
Merko's grandniece, and the Great Merko
was *not* Fred Gibson's grandfather.

"Now," concluded Sally. "Who got
Merko's money—the tall woman or Fred
Gibson?"

Sally wore a smile of triumph as she
looked at Encyclopedia.

The tool shed was still. The boys looked

at their shoes. Had Sally beaten them again? Had Encyclopedia met his master?

Encyclopedia had five short minutes to solve the brain-twister.

Slowly the minutes ticked away. One ... two ... three ... four....

Encyclopedia stirred on his orange crate. He opened his eyes. He smiled at Sally.

"You told it very cleverly," he said. "I nearly said the wrong person. But the answer is really quite simple."

Encyclopedia rose to leave. "The Great Merko's money went to Fred Gibson."

WHY DID ENCYCLOPEDIA SAY THAT?

(Turn to page 185 for the solution to The Case of Merko's Grandson.)

The Case of the Bank Robber

"Three dollars and fifty cents!" exclaimed Encyclopedia, as he finished counting the money in the treasury of the Brown Detective Agency. "Business is booming."

"You should put that money in a bank," said Sally Kimball, whom Encyclopedia had made his bodyguard and junior partner. "Money isn't safe in a shoe box."

"Maybe you're right," said Encyclopedia. "Sometimes even shoes aren't safe in a shoe box. It would look awful if a detective agency was robbed!"

The partners talked it over. They decided

to take the money downtown to a bank and start a savings account.

It was too far to ride on their bicycles, so they took the bus. They got off near the Corning National Bank on Beech Street. As they stepped out of the bus, they heard the sound of shooting.

At first Encyclopedia thought the bus had backfired. A moment later he saw a man in the doorway of the bank.

The man wore a hat. A handkerchief covered the lower part of his face. In one hand he held a yellow paper bag. With the other he waved a gun.

Somebody shouted, "Holdup! Holdup!" Then, all at once, everybody was running, trying to get out of the robber's way.

The man with the gun turned and fled. In his haste he did not seem to look where he was going. He ran into a beggar wearing dark glasses and carrying a white cane and tin cup.

The beggar's cane and cup flew into the

street. The robber and the beggar fell to the sidewalk. They rolled about together for a few seconds before the robber broke away and got to his feet.

He raced down the street just as a police car drew up before the bank. Chief Brown and one of his officers leaped out of the car and ran after the robber.

"We caught him," said Chief Brown at dinner that night. "He led us a merry chase, but we got him. The trouble is we can't charge him with the robbery."

"But why not?" Mrs. Brown demanded.

"Yes, Dad, why not?" Encyclopedia

asked. "Wasn't the money he stole in that yellow paper bag he was carrying?"

Chief Brown laid down his fork. "Do you know what we found in that yellow bag of his? Money? No. A loaf of white bread! He resisted police officers, but I don't know how long we can keep him in jail."

"Are you sure you caught the right man, Dad?" Encyclopedia said.

"We'll have a hard time proving it," said Chief Brown. "No one can identify him. And nobody saw the robber's face. He wore a handkerchief over his nose and mouth and his hat was pulled down over his forehead and eyes. This man we picked up is wearing a brown suit, and the teller at the bank says the robber wore a suit the same color. And, of course, there is the yellow bag. But where's the money?"

"Does the man you picked up have any distinguishing features?" Encyclopedia wanted to know.

"Well, he has a pug nose and a scar running down one cheek. But remember, no one saw the robber's face," said Chief Brown. "I can hold him in jail overnight for resisting a police officer. That's about all."

"I never saw a beggar in Idaville before today," said Encyclopedia thoughtfully.

"Oh, the blind man," said Chief Brown. "He seems like a nice old fellow. He calls himself 'Blind Tom.' I hated to tell him it's against the law to beg here."

"The poor man," said Mrs. Brown. "Won't the Salvation Army help him?"

"Yes," replied Chief Brown. "But he said he likes being on his own. He promised to leave town tomorrow."

"Where is he staying?" asked Encyclopedia.

"At the old Martin Inn," answered Chief Brown. "One of those buildings in the row down by the railroad tracks. Why do you ask? Have you got an idea about this case, Leroy?"

"No," mumbled Encyclopedia.

Mrs. Brown looked hurt. She had come to expect her son to solve a case before dessert.

After dinner, Encyclopedia walked over to Sally's house. "I have to work this evening," he said. "I may need you. Want to come?"

"Oh, boy, do I!" Sally sang out.

The sky was growing dark as the two detectives rode their bicycles down a dingy block west of the railroad station.

"Who lives *here?*" asked Sally as Encyclopedia stopped in front of a run-down hotel.

"Blind Tom, the beggar. He'll be leaving town tomorrow. That's why we have to see him this evening."

"Do you think he can help us?" asked Sally.

"I think so. A blind man sees with his hands," replied Encyclopedia. "Remember how the beggar rolled with the robber on the sidewalk? If he *felt* the robber's face through the handkerchief, he might know him again."

"I get it," said Sally. "If he could feel the man's face again, he might know whether the man your father caught is really the robber!"

"Right," answered Encyclopedia.

"Gosh," said Sally, "I hope he hasn't left town yet!"

Inside the hotel, the desk clerk gave the two young detectives some help. Blind Tom lived alone. His room was Number 214.

Sally and Encyclopedia climbed the dark, creaky stairs to the second floor. They knocked on the door numbered 214. Nobody answered.

"Look, the door's not shut," whispered Sally. "Shall I—"

Encyclopedia nodded.

Sally pushed the door till it swung open so that they could look into the room.

The room was small and shabby. Against the far wall stood an iron bed. A small reading lamp cast its light upon a copy of the *Idaville Daily News* that lay open on the pillow.

Suddenly the tapping of a cane sounded in the hall. Tap . . . tap . . . tap. . . .

Blind Tom came up behind Sally.

"Is someone here?" he asked. "I haven't had a visitor in a long time. I wasn't expecting anyone tonight, but it's nice to have you." He lifted his cane. "Won't you come in?"

"No, thanks!" said Encyclopedia. He pushed Sally down the hall and hurried her down the stairs.

She didn't have a chance to catch her breath until they were outside the hotel.

"Why the big rush?" Sally asked. "I thought you were going to ask Blind Tom if he could recognize the man who robbed the bank this afternoon."

"I don't have to ask him," replied Encyclopedia. "Blind Tom knows the robber, because Blind Tom helped in the robbery!"

HOW DID ENCYCLOPEDIA KNOW THIS?

(See the opposite page for the solution to The Case of the Bank Robber.)

Solution to *The Case of Merko's Grandson*

Both the tall woman and Fred Gibson spoke the truth. Although the Great Merko was not his grandfather, Fred Gibson was the Great Merko's grandson.

The Great Merko, as Encyclopedia realized, was a woman. She was Fred Gibson's *grandmother!*

Solution to *The Case of the Bank Robber*

Blind Tom was not expecting any visitors, he said. He also said that he had not had any visitors "in a long time." Yet the light in his room was on, and a newspaper lay on the pillow.

A blind man does not need a light, and he cannot read a newspaper. So Blind Tom was not blind at all.

Encyclopedia knew then why the beggar had not stepped out of the way of the bank robber. The two men had rolled on the sidewalk together with a purpose—to exchange yellow paper bags!

Blind Tom had slipped the robber the bag holding the loaf of bread, in order to fool the police if they caught him. The robber had slipped Blind Tom the bag holding the money.

Encyclopedia used a telephone in the store on the corner to call his father. Chief Brown hurried to the hotel. He found the money, still in the yellow paper bag, hidden under the mattress of Blind Tom's bed.

Blind Tom and the man the police were holding in jail confessed they had robbed the bank.

Were you able to solve the mysteries? Would you like more of the same? If so, there are eight more cases in *Encyclopedia Brown, Boy Detective,* the book from which these stories came. And there are more than a dozen other Encyclopedia Brown books that will give you a chance to test your detective skills.

Girls Can, Too!
by Lee Bennett Hopkins

Tony said: "Boys are better!
They can . . .

    whack a ball,
    ride a bike with one hand
    leap off a wall."

I just listened
    and when he was through,
I laughed and said:

    "Oh, yeah! Well, girls can, too!"

Then I leaped off the wall,
    and rode away
With *his* 200 baseball cards
    I won that day.

No Girls Allowed
by Jack Prelutsky

When we're playing tag
and the girls want to play,
we yell and we scream
and we chase them away.

When we're playing stickball
or racing our toys
and the girls ask to join,
we say, "Only for boys."

We play hide-and-go-seek
and the girls wander near.
They say, "Please let us hide."
We pretend not to hear.

We don't care for girls
so we don't let them in,
we think that they're dumb—
and besides, they might win.

186

Me

by Karla Kuskin

"My nose is blue,
My teeth are green,
My face is like a soup tureen.
I look just like a lima bean.
I'm very, very lovely.
My feet are far too short
And long.
My hands are left and right
And wrong.
My voice is like the hippo's song.
I'm very, very,
Very, very,
Very, very
Lovely?"

To Be Answered in Our Next Issue

author unknown

When a great tree falls
And people aren't near,
Does it make a noise
If no one can hear?
And which came first,
The hen or the egg?

This impractical question
We ask and then beg.
Some wise men say
It's beyond their ken.
Did anyone ever
Ask the hen?

Homework

by Russell Hoban

Homework sits on top of Sunday, squashing Sunday flat.
Homework has the smell of Monday, homework's very fat.
Heavy books and piles of paper, answers I don't know.
Sunday evening's almost finished, now I'm going to go
Do my homework in the kitchen. Maybe just a snack,
Then I'll sit right down and start as soon as I run back
For some chocolate sandwich cookies. Then I'll really do
All that homework in a minute. First I'll see what new
Show they've got on television in the living room.
Everybody's laughing there, but misery and gloom
And a full refrigerator are where I am at.
I'll just have another sandwich. Homework's very fat.

The Night of the Jack-O'-Lantern

from *Ramona and Her Father*
by Beverly Cleary

The Quimby family has a big problem. Mr. Quimby
has lost his job, and everyone is worried and cross.
Seven-year-old Ramona does her best to make people
smile, but it isn't easy. Her older sister Beatrice, who
is always called Beezus, has become a real grouch.
Even Picky-picky, the family cat, stalks around angrily.

❧ ❧ ❧

"Please pass the tommmy-toes," said
Ramona, hoping to make someone in the
family smile. She felt good when her father
smiled as he passed her the bowl of stewed
tomatoes. He smiled less and less as the days
went by and he had not found work. Too
often he was just plain cross. Ramona had
learned not to rush home from school and
ask, "Did you find a job today, Daddy?" Mrs.
Quimby always seemed to look anxious these
days, either over the cost of groceries or
money the family owed. Beezus had turned
into a regular old grouch, because she
dreaded Creative Writing and perhaps
because she had reached that difficult age
Mrs. Quimby was always talking about,
although Ramona found this hard to believe.

Even Picky-picky was not himself. He lashed his tail and stalked angrily away from his dish when Beezus served him Puss-puddy, the cheapest brand of cat food Mrs. Quimby could find in the market.

All this worried Ramona. She wanted her father to smile and joke, her mother to look happy, her sister to be cheerful, and Picky-picky to eat his food, wash his whiskers, and purr the way he used to.

"And so," Mr. Quimby was saying, "at the end of the interview for the job, the man said he would let me know if anything turned up."

Mrs. Quimby sighed. "Let's hope you hear from him. Oh, by the way, the car has been making a funny noise. A sort of *tappety-tappety* sound."

"It's Murphy's Law," said Mr. Quimby. "Anything that can go wrong will."

Ramona knew her father was not joking this time. Last week, when the washing machine refused to work, the Quimbys had been horrified by the size of the repair bill.

"I like tommy-toes," said Ramona, hoping her little joke would work a second time. This was not exactly true, but she was willing to sacrifice truth for a smile.

Since no one paid any attention, Ramona spoke louder as she lifted the bowl of stewed tomatoes. "Does anybody want any tommy-toes?" she asked. The bowl tipped. Mrs. Quimby silently reached over and wiped spilled juice from the table with her napkin.

Crestfallen, Ramona set the bowl down. No
one had smiled.

"Ramona," said Mr. Quimby, "my
grandmother used to have a saying. 'First
time is funny, second time is silly, third time
is a spanking.' "

Ramona looked down at her place mat.
Nothing seemed to go right lately. Picky-picky
must have felt the same way. He sat down
beside Beezus and meowed his crossest meow.

Mr. Quimby lit a cigarette and asked his
older daughter, "Haven't you fed that cat yet?"

Beezus rose to clear the table. "It
wouldn't do any good. He hasn't eaten his
breakfast. He won't eat that cheap
Puss-puddy."

"Too bad about him." Mr. Quimby blew a cloud of smoke toward the ceiling.

"He goes next door and mews as if we never give him anything to eat," said Beezus. "It's embarrassing."

"He'll just have to learn to eat what we can afford," said Mr. Quimby. "Or we will get rid of him."

This statement shocked Ramona. Picky-picky had been a member of the family since before she was born.

"Well, I don't blame him," said Beezus, picking up the cat and pressing her cheek against his fur. "Puss-puddy stinks."

Mr. Quimby ground out his cigarette.

"Guess what?" said Mrs. Quimby, as if to change the subject. "Howie's grandmother drove out to visit her sister, who lives on a farm, and her sister sent in a lot of pumpkins for jack-o'-lanterns for the neighborhood children. Mrs. Kemp gave us a big one, and it's down in the basement now, waiting to be carved."

"Me! Me!" cried Ramona. "Let me get it!"

"Let's give it a real scary face," said Beezus, no longer difficult.

"I'll have to sharpen my knife," said Mr. Quimby.

"Run along and bring it up, Ramona," said Mrs. Quimby with a real smile.

Relief flooded through Ramona. Her family had returned to normal. She snapped on the basement light, thumped down the stairs, and there in the shadow of the furnace pipes, which reached out like ghostly arms, was a big, round pumpkin. Ramona grasped its scratchy stem, found the pumpkin too big to lift that way, bent over, hugged it in both arms, and raised it from the cement floor. The pumpkin was heavier than she had expected, and she must not let it drop and smash all over the concrete floor.

"Need some help, Ramona?" Mrs. Quimby called down the stairs.

"I can do it." Ramona felt for each step with her feet and emerged, victorious, into the kitchen.

"Wow! That *is* a big one." Mr. Quimby was sharpening his jackknife on a whetstone while Beezus and her mother hurried through the dishes.

"A pumpkin that size would cost a lot at the market," Mrs. Quimby remarked. "A couple of dollars, at least."

"Let's give it eyebrows like last year," said Ramona.

"And ears," said Beezus.

"And lots of teeth," added Ramona.

There would be no jack-o'-lantern with one tooth and three triangles for eyes and nose in the Quimbys' front window on Halloween. Mr. Quimby was the best pumpkin carver on Klickitat Street. Everybody knew that.

"Hmm. Let's see now." Mr. Quimby studied the pumpkin, turning it to find the best side for the face. "I think the nose should go about here." With a pencil he sketched a nose-shaped nose, not a triangle, while his daughters leaned on their elbows to watch.

"Shall we have it smile or frown?" he asked.

"Smile!" said Ramona, who had had enough of frowning.

"Frown!" said Beezus.

The mouth turned up on one side and down on the other. Eyes were sketched and eyebrows. "Very expressive," said Mr. Quimby. "Something between a leer and a sneer." He cut a circle around the top of the pumpkin and lifted it off for a lid.

Without being asked, Ramona found a big spoon for scooping out the seeds.

Picky-picky came into the kitchen to see if something beside Puss-puddy had been placed in his dish. When he found that it had not, he paused, sniffed the unfamiliar pumpkin smell, and with his tail twitching angrily stalked out of the kitchen. Ramona was glad Beezus did not notice.

"If we don't let the candle burn the jack-o'-lantern, we can have pumpkin pie," said Mrs. Quimby. "I can even freeze some of the pumpkin for Thanksgiving."

Mr. Quimby began to whistle as he carved with skill and care, first a mouthful of teeth, each one neat and square, then eyes and jagged, ferocious eyebrows. He was working on two ears shaped like question marks, when Mrs. Quimby said, "Bedtime, Ramona."

"I am going to stay up until Daddy finishes," Ramona informed her family. "No ifs, ands, or buts."

"Run along and take your bath," said Mrs. Quimby, "and you can watch awhile longer."

Because her family was happy once more, Ramona did not protest. She returned quickly, however, still damp under her pajamas, to see what her father had thought of next. Hair, that's what he had thought of, something he could carve because the pumpkin was so big. He cut a few C-shaped curls around the hole in the top of the pumpkin before he reached inside and hollowed out a candle holder in the bottom.

"There," he said and rinsed his jackknife under the kitchen faucet. "A work of art."

Mrs. Quimby found a candle stub, inserted it in the pumpkin, lit it, and set the lid in place. Ramona switched off the light. The jack-o'-lantern leered and sneered with a flickering flame.

"Oh, Daddy!" Ramona threw her arms around her father. "It's the wickedest jack-o'-lantern in the whole world."

Mr. Quimby kissed the top of Ramona's head. "Thank you. I take that as a compliment. Now run along to bed."

Ramona could tell by the sound of her father's voice that he was smiling. She ran off to her room without thinking up excuses for staying up just five more minutes, added a postscript to her prayers thanking God for the big pumpkin, and another asking him to find her father a job, and fell asleep at once, not bothering to tuck her panda bear in beside her for comfort.

In the middle of the night Ramona found herself suddenly awake without knowing why she was awake. Had she heard a noise? Yes, she had. Tense, she listened hard. There it was again, a sort of thumping, scuffling noise, not very loud but there just the same. Silence. Then she heard it again. Inside the house. In the kitchen. Something was in the kitchen, and it was moving.

Ramona's mouth was so dry she could barely whisper, "Daddy!" No answer. More thumping. Someone bumped against the wall. Someone, something was coming to get them. Ramona thought about the leering, sneering face on the kitchen table. All the ghost stories she had ever heard, all the ghostly pictures she had ever seen flew through her mind. Could the jack-o'-lantern have come to life? Of course not. It was only a pumpkin, but still— A bodyless, leering head was too horrifying to think about.

Ramona sat up in bed and shrieked, "Daddy!"

A light came on in her parents' room, feet thumped to the floor, Ramona's tousled father in rumpled pajamas was silhouetted in Ramona's doorway, followed by her mother tugging a robe on over her short nightgown.

"What is it, Baby?" asked Mr. Quimby. Both Ramona's parents called her Baby when they were worried about her, and tonight Ramona was so relieved to see them she did not mind.

"Was it a bad dream?" asked Mrs. Quimby.

"Th-there's something in the kitchen." Ramona's voice quavered.

Beezus, only half-awake, joined the family. "What's happening?" she asked. "What's going on?"

"There's something in the kitchen," said Ramona, feeling braver. "Something moving."

"Sh-h!" commanded Mr. Quimby.

Tense, the family listened to silence.

"You just had a bad dream." Mrs. Quimby came into the room, kissed Ramona, and started to tuck her in.

Ramona pushed the blanket away. "It was *not* a bad dream," she insisted. "I did too hear something. Something spooky."

"All we have to do is look," said Mr. Quimby, reasonable—and bravely, Ramona thought. Nobody would get her into that kitchen.

Ramona waited, scarcely breathing, fearing for her father's safety as he walked down the hall and flipped on the kitchen light. No shout, no yell came from that part of the house. Instead her father laughed, and Ramona felt brave enough to follow the rest of the family to see what was funny.

There was a strong smell of cat food in the kitchen. What Ramona saw, and what Beezus saw, did not strike them as one bit

funny. Their jack-o'-lantern, the
jack-o'-lantern their father had worked so
hard to carve, no longer had a whole face.
Part of its forehead, one ferocious eyebrow,
one eye, and part of its nose were gone,
replaced by a jagged hole edged by little
teeth marks. Picky-picky was crouched in
guilt under the kitchen table.

The nerve of that cat. "Bad cat! Bad
cat!" shrieked Ramona, stamping her bare
foot on the cold linoleum. The old yellow cat
fled to the dining room, where he crouched
under the table, his eyes glittering out of the
darkness.

Mrs. Quimby laughed a small rueful laugh. "I knew he liked canteloupe, but I had no idea he liked pumpkin, too." With a butcher's knife she began to cut up the remains of the jack-o'-lantern, carefully removing, Ramona noticed, the parts with teeth marks.

"I *told* you he wouldn't eat that awful Puss-puddy." Beezus was accusing her father of denying their cat. "Of course he had to eat our jack-o'-lantern. He's starving."

"Beezus, dear," said Mrs. Quimby. "We simply cannot afford the brand of food Picky-picky used to eat. Now be reasonable."

Beezus was in no mood to be reasonable. "Then how come Daddy can afford to smoke?" she demanded to know.

Ramona was astonished to hear her sister speak this way to her mother.

Mr. Quimby looked angry. "Young lady," he said, and when he called Beezus young lady, Ramona knew her sister had better watch out. "Young lady, I've heard enough about that old tom cat and his food. My cigarettes are none of your business."

Ramona expected Beezus to say she was sorry or maybe burst into tears and run to her room. Instead she pulled Picky-picky out from under the table and held him to her chest as if she were shielding him from danger. "They are too my business," she informed her father. "Cigarettes can kill you. Your lungs will turn black and you'll *die!* We made posters about it at school. And besides, cigarettes pollute the air!"

Ramona was horrified by her sister's daring, and at the same time she was a tiny bit pleased. Beezus was usually well-behaved while Ramona was the one who had tantrums. Then she was struck by the meaning of her sister's angry words and was frightened.

"That's enough out of you," Mr. Quimby told Beezus, "and let me remind you that if you had shut that cat in the basement as you were supposed to, this would never have happened."

Mrs. Quimby quietly stowed the remains of the jack-o'-lantern in a plastic bag in the refrigerator.

Beezus opened the basement door and gently set Picky-picky on the top step. "Night-night," she said tenderly.

"Young lady," began Mr. Quimby. Young lady again! Now Beezus was really going to catch it. "You are getting altogether too big for your britches lately. Just be careful how you talk around this house."

Still Beezus did not say she was sorry. She did not burst into tears. She simply stalked off to her room.

Ramona was the one who burst into tears. She didn't mind when she and Beezus quarreled. She even enjoyed a good fight now and then to clear the air, but she could not bear it when anyone else in the family quarreled, and those awful things Beezus said—were they true?

"Don't cry, Ramona." Mrs. Quimby put her arm around her younger daughter. "We'll get another pumpkin."

"B-but it won't be as big," sobbed Ramona, who wasn't crying about the pumpkin at all. She was crying about important things like her father being cross so much now that he wasn't working and his lungs turning black and Beezus being so disagreeable when before she had always been so polite (to grown-ups) and anxious to do the right thing.

"Come on, let's all go to bed and things will look brighter in the morning," said Mrs. Quimby.

"In a few minutes." Mr. Quimby picked up a package of cigarettes he had left on the kitchen table, shook one out, lit it, and sat down, still looking angry.

Were his lungs turning black this very minute? Ramona wondered. How would anybody know, when his lungs were inside him? She let her mother guide her to her room and tuck her in bed.

"Now don't worry about your jack-o'-lantern. We'll get another pumpkin. It won't be as big, but you'll have your jack-o'-lantern." Mrs. Quimby kissed Ramona good-night.

"Nighty-night," said Ramona in a muffled voice. As soon as her mother left, she hopped out of bed and pulled her old panda bear out from under the bed and tucked it under the covers beside her for comfort. The bear must have been dusty because Ramona sneezed.

"Gesundheit!" said Mr. Quimby, passing by her door. "We'll carve another jack-o'-lantern tomorrow. Don't worry." He was not angry with Ramona.

Ramona snuggled down with her dusty bear. Didn't grown-ups think children worried about anything but jack-o'-lanterns? Didn't they know children worried about grown-ups?

Ramona and Beezus think up a great plan to get their father to quit smoking—as you will discover when you read the rest of *Ramona and Her Father*. And if you liked this story, you will want to read others of the more than twenty books Beverly Cleary has written, such as *Ramona the Brave, Henry and Ribsy*, and *Henry and Beezus*.

I Know an Old Lady
Who Swallowed a Fly

an old folksong

I know an old lady who swallowed a fly.
I don't know why she swallowed a fly.
Perhaps she'll die.

I know an old lady who swallowed a spider,
That wriggled and jiggled and tickled inside her.
She swallowed the spider to catch the fly.
I don't know why she swallowed the fly.
Perhaps she'll die.

I know an old lady who swallowed a bird.
How absurd to swallow a bird.
She swallowed the bird to catch the spider
That wriggled and jiggled and tickled inside her.
She swallowed the spider to catch the fly.
I don't know why she swallowed the fly.
Perhaps she'll die.

I know an old lady who swallowed a cat.
Imagine that! She swallowed a cat!
She swallowed the cat to catch the bird.
She swallowed the bird to catch the spider
That wriggled and jiggled and tickled inside her.
She swallowed the spider to catch the fly.
I don't know why she swallowed the fly.
Perhaps she'll die.

I know an old lady who swallowed a dog.
Oh what a hog to swallow a dog.
She swallowed the dog to catch the cat.
She swallowed the cat to catch the bird.
She swallowed the bird to catch the spider
That wriggled and jiggled and tickled inside her.
She swallowed the spider to catch the fly.
I don't know why she swallowed the fly.
Perhaps she'll die.

I know an old lady who swallowed a goat.
Opened her throat and swallowed a goat.
She swallowed the goat to catch the dog.
She swallowed the dog to catch the cat.
She swallowed the cat to catch the bird.
She swallowed the bird to catch the spider
That wriggled and jiggled and tickled inside her.
She swallowed the spider to catch the fly.
I don't know why she swallowed the fly.
Perhaps she'll die.

I know an old lady who swallowed a cow.
I don't know how she swallowed a cow.
She swallowed the cow to catch the goat.
She swallowed the goat to catch the dog.
She swallowed the dog to catch the cat.
She swallowed the cat to catch the bird.
She swallowed the bird to catch the spider
That wriggled and jiggled and tickled inside her.
She swallowed the spider to catch the fly.
I don't know why she swallowed the fly.
Perhaps she'll die.

I know an old lady who swallowed a horse.
She died, of course!

One Morning in Maine

written and illustrated by Robert McCloskey

One morning in Maine, Sal woke up. She peeked over
the top of the covers. The bright sunlight made her
blink, so she pulled the covers up and was just about to
go back to sleep when she remembered "today is the
day I am going to Buck's Harbor with my father!"

Sal pushed back the covers, hopped out of bed, put
on her robe and slippers, and hurried out into the hall.

There was little Jane, just coming out of her room.

Sister Jane had wiggled out of her nightie, so Sal helped her put on her robe and slippers. "You don't want to catch cold and have to stay in bed, Jane, because this morning we are going to Buck's Harbor," Sal reminded her sister.

Together they went into the bathroom to get ready for breakfast. Sal squeezed out toothpaste on sister Jane's brush and said, "Be careful, Jane, and don't get it in your hair."

Then she squeezed some toothpaste on her own brush and when she started to brush her teeth something felt *very strange! One of her teeth felt loose!* She wiggled it with her tongue, then she wiggled it with her finger.

"Oh, dear!" thought Sal. "This *cannot* be true!"

Standing on the stool, she looked in the mirror and wiggled her tooth again. Sure enough, it was loose! You could even *see* it wiggle.

"Ma-a-a-ma!" she cried. "One of my teeth is loose! It

will hurt and I'll have to stay in bed! I won't be able to eat my breakfast and go with Daddy to Buck's Harbor!" She came running down the stairs and into the kitchen.

"Why, Sal," said her mother, "that's nothing to worry about. That means that today you've become a big girl. Everybody's baby teeth get loose and come out when they grow up. A nice new bigger and better tooth will grow in when this one comes out."

"Did your baby teeth get loose and come out when you grew to be a big girl?" Sal asked her mother.

"Yes," she answered. "And then these nice large ones grew in. When Penny grew to be a big dog, his puppy teeth dropped out too."

"And will Jane's get loose too?" asked Sal.

"Yes," said her mother. "But not for a long time, not until she stops being a baby and grows up to be a big girl like you. Jane is so young that she hasn't even grown all her baby teeth yet. Now let's all go upstairs and brush our hair and get dressed for breakfast."

"It feels so different to be a big girl and have a loose tooth," said Sal, "especially when you are chewing. When is it going to come out?"

"Perhaps today, perhaps tomorrow," answered her mother. "But when your tooth does come out, you put it under your pillow and make a wish, and your wish is supposed to come true."

"I know what I'm going to wish for!" said Sal. "A nice cold choco—"

"But you mustn't tell anybody your wish, or it won't come true," cautioned her mother. "It's supposed to be a *secret* wish. Now finish your milk, Sal; then you can go out on the beach and help your father dig clams for lunch."

"I'm a big girl, and I can help him dig a lot of clams, fast," said Sal, "so we can hurry up and go to Buck's Harbor."

After breakfast, when Sal went out to help her
father, she saw a fish hawk flying overhead, carrying
a fish.

"I have a loose tooth!" Sal called up to the fish hawk.
The fish hawk flew straight to her nest on top of a
tree without answering. She was too busy feeding
breakfast to her baby fish hawk.

Sal wondered for a moment if the baby fish hawk
had any teeth to chew his breakfast. Then she started
on down toward the beach where her father was
digging clams.

When she came near to the water she saw a loon.

"I have a loose tooth!" Sal called to the loon. "And
today I have started to be a big girl."

217

The loon didn't say anything but kept swimming in circles. Then he ducked his beak in the water and snapped out a herring. Then he swallowed it *whole*, without a single chew.

"Perhaps loons don't have teeth," thought Sal, and

she was just turning to go on her way when a seal
poked his head up out of the water.

"I have a loose tooth!" Sal said to the seal, and the
seal, being just as curious as most seals, swam nearer
to have a good look.

"See?" said Sal, and she walked closer, right down
onto the slippery seaweeds at the water's edge.

The seal swam nearer, and Sal was stooping nearer
when O-O-Oops! she slipped on the seaweed and fell
kasploosh!

The seal disappeared beneath the water and the loon
laughed, "Luh-hoo-hoo-hoo-hoo-hooh!"

Sal wasn't hurt a bit, so she laughed too, then she
got up carefully and started on down the shore to help
her father dig clams.

She paused to watch some sea gulls having
breakfast. They were dropping mussels down on a rock
to crack the mussel shells, just like nuts. Then they
flew down to eat the insides.

220

"Do sea gulls have teeth?" wondered Sal as she wiggled her own loose one with her tongue. She thought of her secret wish and smiled, then hurried down the beach to where she could see her father.

"Daddy! I have a loose tooth!" she shouted. "And when it drops out I'm going to put it under my pillow and wish a wish. You can even see it wiggle!"

Her father stopped digging clams to watch while Sal wiggled her tooth for him. "You're growing into a big girl when you get a loose tooth!" he said. "What are you going to wish for when it drops out?"

"I can't tell you that," said Sal solemnly, "because it's supposed to be a *secret* wish."

"Oh, yes, so it is," her father agreed.

"May I help you dig clams?" Sal asked.

"I'm almost finished," he replied, "but you can help if you like. First, you must take off your shoes and socks, and roll up your pants too, so that they won't get all wet and muddy."

Sal took off her shoes and socks and put them on a dry rock. She rolled up her pants and waded into the muddy gravel to help her father. He dug in the mud with his clam rake, and then they looked carefully and felt around in the muddy hole for clams.

"I found a tiny baby one!" said Sal.

"You certainly did," said her father. "But it's too small. We just keep the large ones, like this. Let's put the baby clam back in the mud so he can grow to be a big clam someday."

"He *is* such a baby clam, and I guess he *is* too small," she agreed.

"I guess he isn't even big enough to have all his baby teeth," said Sal, placing the tiny clam tenderly back in the mud.

"Clams don't have teeth," grunted her father, digging another rakeful of mud.

"Not even big clams have teeth?" asked Sal.

"Not even big clams," her father assured her.

"Do baby fish hawks and big fish hawks have teeth?" asked Sal.

"No," said her father.

"Do loons have teeth?" she asked, "and gulls?"

"No."

"Do seals have teeth?"

"Yes, they have 'em," he answered.

"And do their teeth get loose like this?" asked Sal, opening her mouth to show her loose tooth.

"O-owh!" she said with great surprise. She felt with her tongue, and she felt with her muddy fingers.

"Why it's *gone!*" she said sadly, feeling once more just to make sure. The loose tooth was really and truly gone. The salty mud from her fingers tasted bitter, and she made a bitter-tasting face that was almost a face like crying.

"Did you swallow it, Sal?" her father asked with a concerned smile.

"No." She shook her head sadly. "I was too busy asking to do any swallowing. It just dropped itself out. It's gone, and I can't put it under my pillow and make my wish come true!"

"That's too bad," her father sympathized. "But you are growing into a big girl, and big girls don't cry about a little thing like that. They wait for another tooth to come loose and make a wish on that one."

"Maybe we can find my tooth where it dropped," said Sal, hopefully feeling around in the muddy gravel where the clams live.

Sal's father helped her look, but a muddy tooth looks so much like a muddy pebble, and a muddy pebble looks so much like a muddy tooth, that they hunted and hunted without finding it.

"We'll have to stop looking and take our clams back to the house, Sal," her father said at last, "or we won't have time for the trip to the village." He washed off the clams in the clean salt water of the bay, and Sal reluctantly stopped looking and waded in to wash the mud from her feet and hands.

"I guess some clam will find my tooth and get what I wished for," said Sal. "If we come back here tomorrow and find a clam eating a chocolate ice-cream cone, why, we'll have to take it away from him and make him give my tooth back too," she said.

While Sal put on her socks and shoes her father packed seaweed around the clams to keep them moist and fresh.

"Now, let's hurry back to the house," he said, "and in a few minutes we'll be on our way to Buck's Harbor in the boat to get milk and groceries."

"Okay," Sal answered, scrambling to her feet.

She gave one last look at the muddy place where she'd lost her tooth and then started walking back along the shore with her father. She walked along slowly, looking at her feet so that her father could not see her face, in case it looked almost like crying.

"Oh! See what I've found!" she exclaimed, stooping to pick up a feather.

"It's a gull's feather," said her father, pausing for Sal to pick it up.

"Did a gull lose it? Will another feather grow in where this one dropped out?" asked Sal.

"Yes, Sal, that's right," answered her father.

"Maybe sea gulls put dropped-out feathers under their pillows and wish secret wishes," Sal suggested.

"Sea gulls don't use pillows, but I suppose they can make wishes," her father said.

"Then I'll make my wish on this *feather*," Sal decided.

"Perhaps the sea gull has already made a wish on that feather and the wish is used up," suggested her father.

"Oh, no," Sal said definitely, "he didn't, you see. I guess because he was too busy flying and not looking back. He didn't notice it was loose when he brushed his feathers this morning, so he didn't expect it would drop out. He doesn't even know it's gone," she convinced herself. She closed her eyes tight and wished her secret wish.

When they reached home Sal's mother and sister Jane were waiting with a box of empty milk bottles to return to the store and a list of things to buy.

"I'll have a nice clam chowder ready for your lunch

when you get back," said Sal's mother, waving
good-by.

"I'll take good care of Jane," Sal promised. "I'm a
big girl and I can watch so she doesn't tumble into the
water."

Sal and Jane and their father went down to the
shore and got aboard their boat.

Sal and Jane put on their life preservers while their
father prepared to start the outboard motor. He pulled
and he pulled on the rope to start it, but the outboard
motor just coughed and sputtered and wouldn't start.

So he had to row the boat all the way across the bay
to Buck's Harbor where the store was.

The harbor was full of boats, and Sal's father rowed
their boat among them, up to a landing, and tied it so
it would not drift away while they were at the store.
They all climbed ashore, and Sal's father brought along
the milk bottles. He brought the outboard motor too, so
Mr. Condon who ran the garage could fix it.

As they came up the path to the village Mr. Condon was outside his garage, putting gas into a car.

"I have a tooth out!" Sal greeted. "And our outboard motor won't run."

"My, such trouble!" Mr. Condon commented, and after he had admired the empty place where Sal's tooth was missing they took the outboard motor into the garage to find why it wouldn't run. Mr. Condon pinched a little with his pliers, tunked a bit with his hammer, and then, after selecting a large wrench, he took out the spark plug.

"Came right out, just like that tooth of yours, didn't it, Sal?" he said, holding it up to the light. "Humph!" he grunted, tossing it on the floor. "Needs a new plug!"

Sal was just about to ask how long it would take for a new spark plug to grow in when Mr. Condon reached

up on the shelf and picked out a brand-new one, and put it in the motor.

Sal picked up the old spark plug and handed it to sister Jane. Jane was so little that she didn't understand about secret wishes. Jane was so little that she couldn't even say ice-cream cone! So Sal wished the secret wish for Jane on the spark plug.

Mr. Condon pulled the rope, and the motor started right up, just as good as new. Sal's father thanked him and picked up the motor and the milk bottles. Jane carried her spark plug, Sal carried her feather, and they said good-by and walked across the street to where Mr. Condon's brother kept store.

"Well, look who's here!" said the Mr. Condon who kept store.

"I have a tooth out!" Sal shouted, returning Mr. Condon's greeting.

She showed the empty place where her tooth had been, first to Mr. Condon, then to Mr. Ferd Clifford and Mr. Oscar Staples, who were sitting in the store talking about trapping lobsters and how the fish were biting.

"Don't put your tongue in the empty place," Mr. Clifford advised, "and a nice shiny gold one like mine will grow in."

"But I didn't know soon enough," said Sal, looking confused.

"Hawh!" said Mr. Condon, chuckling. "Don't you go worryin' about everything these jokers suggest. I don't suppose," he added, opening up his freezer, "that you could eat an ice-cream cone with one of your teeth out?"

"Oh, yes, I could!" said Sal. "And it's supposed to be chocolate!"

"And this little lady?" he questioned, turning to Jane.

"Hers is supposed to be vanilla, so the drips won't spot, and you'd better push it together tight, so it won't drop off," Sal dictated, "because she's still almost a baby and doesn't even have all of her first teeth."

After Mr. Condon had put the groceries and milk in the box, they thanked him once more and waved good-by. They walked down the path to the harbor and down the runway to the float where their boat was tied. They all climbed aboard, carrying the outboard

motor, the box of milk and groceries, the feather, the spark plug, and the ice-cream cones.

While their father fastened the outboard motor to the boat Sal and Jane finished their ice-cream cones.

"I want s'more!" Jane demanded.

"Silly!" exclaimed Sal. "Our wishes are all used up." Then she remembered that she was growing up, and just like a grownup she said, "Besides, Jane, two ice-cream cones would ruin your appetite. When we get home we're going to have CLAM CHOWDER FOR LUNCH!"

Sal has other adventures in *Blueberries for Sal*, which is also by Robert McCloskey. In this story, Sal and her mother go to pick blueberries in the Maine woods and meet a mother bear and her cub.

A Big Deal for the Tooth Fairy
by X. J. Kennedy

Tooth Fairy, hear! Tonight's the night
   I've dreamed about for ages,
For haven't we kids got a right
   To rake in living wages?

I've tried to work my back teeth loose,
   Tied doorknobs (threads—what cop-outs!),
But gosh! my jaws just won't produce
   A quick cash crop of dropouts.

So come prepared to lose a heap
   In larger trading ventures.
Tonight I lay me down to sleep
   On top of Grandpop's dentures.

In the Motel
by X. J. Kennedy

Bouncing! bouncing! on the beds
My brother Bob and I cracked heads—

People next door heard the crack,
Whammed on the wall, so we whammed right back.

Dad's razor caused an overload
And wow! did the TV set explode!

Someone's car backed fast and—tinkle!
In our windshield was a wrinkle.

Eight more days on the road? Hooray!
What a bang-up holiday!

If Once You Have Slept on an Island

by Rachel Field

If once you have slept on an island
   You'll never be quite the same;
You may look as you looked the day before
   And go by the same old name,

You may bustle about in street and shop;
   You may sit at home and sew,
But you'll see blue water and wheeling gulls
   Wherever your feet may go.

You may chat with the neighbors of this and that
   And close to your fire keep,
But you'll hear ship whistle and lighthouse bell
   And tides beat through your sleep.

Oh, you won't know why, and you can't say how
   Such change upon you came,
But—once you have slept on an island
   You'll never be quite the same!

The Night Will Never Stay

by Eleanor Farjeon

The night will never stay,
The night will still go by,
Though with a million stars
You pin it to the sky;

Though you bind it with the blowing wind
And buckle it with the moon,
The night will slip away
Like sorrow or a tune.

Questions at Night

by Louis Untermeyer

Why
Is the sky?

What starts the thunder overhead?
Who makes the crashing noise?
Are the angels falling out of bed?
Are they breaking all their toys?

Why does the sun go down so soon?
Why do the night-clouds crawl
Hungrily up to the new-laid moon
And swallow it, shell and all?

If there's a Bear among the stars
As all the people say,
Won't he jump over those Pasture-bars
And drink up the Milky Way?

Does every star that happens to fall
Turn into a fire-fly?
Can't it ever get back to Heaven at all?
And why
Is the sky?

Firefly
by Elizabeth Madox Roberts

A little light is going by,
Is going up to see the sky,
A little light with wings.

I never could have thought of it,
To have a little bug all lit
And made to go on wings.

Night
by Sara Teasdale

Stars over snow,
   And in the west a planet
Swinging below a star—
   Look for a lovely thing and you will find it,
It is not far—
   It never will be far.

A wolf
I considered myself
but
the owls are hooting
and
the night I fear.

an Osage Indian song

The Falling Star
by Sara Teasdale

I saw a star slide down the sky,
Blinding the north as it went by,
Too burning and too quick to hold,
Too lovely to be bought or sold,
Good only to make wishes on
And then forever to be gone.

The owl hooted,
Telling of the morning star.
He hooted again,
Announcing the dawn.

a Yuma Indian song

Quoits
by Mary Effie Lee Newsome

In wintertime I have such fun
　When I play quoits with father.
I beat him almost every game.
　He never seems to bother.

He looks at mother and just smiles.
　All this seems strange to me,
For when he plays with grown-up folks,
　He beats them easily.

Quibble
by Eve Merriam

U can be seen without a Q.
But Q must always go with U.

I think it's queer
And not quite right.

So here is a Q all on its own.
Come on, Q. Stand up alone.
U keep out.

Alas, poor Q feels qivery, qavery,
Qietly sick . . .

Hurry back, U,
To the rescue—quick!

A Bear Called Paddington

from *A Bear Called Paddington* by Michael Bond
with drawings by Peggy Fortnum

Mr. and Mrs. Brown first met Paddington on a railway platform. In fact, that was how he came to have such an unusual name for a bear, for Paddington was the name of the station.

The Browns were there to meet their daughter Judy, who was coming home from school for the holidays. It was a warm summer day and the station was crowded with people on their way to the seaside. Trains were whistling, taxis hooting, porters rushing about shouting at one another, and altogether there was so much noise that Mr. Brown, who saw him first, had to tell his wife several times before she understood.

"A *bear*? On Paddington station?" Mrs. Brown looked at her husband in amazement. "Don't be silly, Henry. There can't be!"

Mr. Brown adjusted his glasses. "But there is," he insisted. "I distinctly saw it. Over there—behind those mailbags. It was wearing a funny kind of hat."

Without waiting for a reply he caught hold of his wife's arm and pushed her through the crowd, round a trolley laden with chocolate and cups of tea, past a bookstall, and through a gap in a pile of suitcases towards the Lost Property Office.

"There you are," he announced, triumphantly, pointing towards a dark corner. "I told you so!"

Mrs. Brown followed the direction of his arm and dimly made out a small, furry object in the shadows. It seemed to be sitting on some kind of suitcase and around its neck there was a label with some writing on it. The suitcase was old and battered and on the side, in large letters, were the words WANTED ON VOYAGE.

Mrs. Brown clutched at her husband. "Why, Henry," she exclaimed. "I believe you were right after all. It *is* a bear!"

She peered at it more closely. It seemed a very unusual kind of bear. It was brown in colour, a rather dirty brown, and it was wearing a most odd-looking hat, with a wide brim, just as Mr. Brown had said. From beneath the brim two large, round eyes stared back at her.

Seeing that something was expected of it the bear stood up and politely raised its hat, revealing two black ears. "Good afternoon," it said, in a small, clear voice.

"Er . . . good afternoon," replied Mr. Brown, doubtfully. There was a moment of silence.

The bear looked at them inquiringly. "Can I help you?"

238

Mr. Brown looked rather embarrassed. "Well...no. Er...as a matter of fact, we were wondering if we could help you."

Mrs. Brown bent down. "You're a very small bear," she said.

The bear puffed out its chest. "I'm a very rare sort of bear," he replied, importantly. "There aren't many of us left where I come from."

"And where is that?" asked Mrs. Brown.

The bear looked round carefully before replying. "Darkest Peru. I'm not really supposed to be here at all. I'm a stowaway!"

"A stowaway?" Mr. Brown lowered his voice and looked anxiously over his shoulder. He almost expected to see a policeman standing behind him with a notebook and pencil, taking everything down.

"Yes," said the bear. "I emigrated, you know." A sad expression came into its eyes. "I used to live with my Aunt Lucy in Peru, but she had to go into a home for retired bears."

"You don't mean to say you've come all the way from South America by yourself?" exclaimed Mrs. Brown.

The bear nodded. "Aunt Lucy always said she wanted me to emigrate when I was old enough. That's why she taught me to speak English."

"But whatever did you do for food?" asked Mr. Brown. "You must be starving."

Bending down, the bear unlocked the suitcase with a small key, which it also had round its neck, and brought out an almost empty glass jar. "I ate marmalade," he said, rather proudly. "Bears like marmalade. And I lived in a lifeboat."

"But what are you going to do now?" said Mr. Brown. "You can't just sit on Paddington station waiting for something to happen."

"Oh, I shall be all right . . . I expect." The bear bent down to do up its case again. As he did so Mrs. Brown caught a glimpse of the writing on the label. It said, simply, PLEASE LOOK AFTER THIS BEAR. THANK YOU.

She turned appealingly to her husband. "Oh, Henry, what *shall* we do? We can't just leave him here. There's no knowing what might happen to him. London's such a big place when you've nowhere to go. Can't he come and stay with us for a few days?"

Mr. Brown hesitated. "But Mary, dear, we can't take him . . . not just like that. After all . . ."

"After all, *what*?" Mrs. Brown's voice had a firm note to it. She looked down at the bear. "He *is* rather sweet. And he'd be such company for Jonathan and Judy. Even if it's only for a little while. They'd never forgive you if they knew you'd left him here."

"It all seems highly irregular," said Mr. Brown, doubtfully. "I'm sure there's a law about it." He bent down. "Would you like to come and stay with us?" he asked. "That is," he added, hastily, not wishing to offend the bear, "if you've nothing else planned."

The bear jumped and his hat nearly fell off with excitement. "Oooh, yes, please. I should like that very much. I've nowhere to go and everyone seems in such a hurry."

"Well, that's settled then," said Mrs. Brown, before her husband could change his mind. "And you can have marmalade for breakfast every morning, and—" she tried hard to think of something else that bears might like.

"*Every* morning?" The bear looked as if it could hardly believe its ears. "I only had it on special occasions at home. Marmalade's very expensive in Darkest Peru."

"Then you shall have it every morning starting tomorrow," continued Mrs. Brown. "And honey on Sunday."

A worried expression came over the bear's face. "Will it cost very much?" he asked. "You see, I haven't very much money."

"Of course not. We wouldn't dream of charging you anything. We shall expect you to be one of the family, shan't we, Henry?" Mrs. Brown looked at her husband for support.

"Of course," said Mr. Brown. "By the way," he added, "if you *are* coming home with us you'd better know our names. This is Mrs. Brown and I'm Mr. Brown."

The bear raised its hat politely—twice. "I haven't really got a name," he said. "Only a Peruvian one which no one can understand."

"Then we'd better give you an English one," said Mrs. Brown. "It'll make things much easier." She looked round the station for inspiration. "It ought to be something special," she said thoughtfully. As she spoke an engine standing in one of the platforms gave a loud whistle and let off a cloud of steam. "I know what!" she exclaimed. "We found you on Paddington station so we'll call you Paddington!"

"Paddington!" The bear repeated it several times to make sure. "It seems a very long name."

"Quite distinguished," said Mr. Brown. "Yes, I like Paddington as a name. Paddington it shall be."

Mrs. Brown stood up. "Good. Now, Paddington, I have to meet our little daughter, Judy, off the train. She's coming home from school. I'm sure you must be thirsty after your long journey, so you go along to the buffet with Mr. Brown and he'll buy you a nice cup of tea."

Paddington licked his lips. "I'm *very* thirsty," he

said. "Sea water makes you thirsty." He picked up his suitcase, pulled his hat down firmly over his head, and waved a paw politely in the direction of the buffet. "After you, Mr. Brown."

"Er . . . thank you, Paddington," said Mr. Brown.

"Now, Henry, look after him," Mrs. Brown called after them. "And for goodness' sake, when you get a moment, take that label off his neck. It makes him look like a parcel. I'm sure he'll get put in a luggage van or something if a porter sees him."

The buffet was crowded when they entered but Mr. Brown managed to find a table for two in a corner. By standing on a chair Paddington could just rest his paws comfortably on the glass top. He looked around with interest while Mr. Brown went to fetch the tea. The sight of everyone eating reminded him of how hungry he felt. There was a half-eaten bun on the table but just as he reached out his paw a waitress came up and swept it into a pan.

"You don't want that, dearie," she said, giving him a friendly pat. "You don't know where it's been."

Paddington felt so empty he didn't really mind where it had been but he was much too polite to say anything.

"Well, Paddington," said Mr. Brown, as he placed two steaming cups of tea on the table and a plate piled high with cakes. "How's that to be going on with?"

Paddington's eyes glistened. "It's very nice, thank you," he exclaimed, eyeing the tea doubtfully. "But it's rather hard drinking out of a cup. I usually get my head stuck, or else my hat falls in and makes it taste nasty."

Mr. Brown hesitated. "Then you'd better give your

hat to me. I'll pour the tea into a saucer for you. It's not really done in the best circles, but I'm sure no one will mind just this once."

Paddington removed his hat and laid it carefully on the table while Mr. Brown poured out the tea. He looked hungrily at the cakes, in particular at a large cream-and-jam one which Mr. Brown placed on a plate in front of him.

"There you are, Paddington," he said. "I'm sorry they haven't any marmalade ones, but they were the best I could get."

"I'm glad I emigrated," said Paddington, as he reached out a paw and pulled the plate nearer. "Do you think anyone would mind if I stood on the table to eat?"

Before Mr. Brown could answer he had climbed up and placed his right paw firmly on the bun. It was a very large bun, the biggest and stickiest Mr. Brown had been able to find, and in a matter of moments most of the inside found its way on to Paddington's whiskers. People started to nudge each other and began staring in their direction. Mr. Brown wished he had chosen a plain, ordinary bun, but he wasn't very experienced in the ways of bears. He stirred his tea and looked out of the window, pretending he had tea with a bear on Paddington station every day of his life.

"Henry!" The sound of his wife's voice brought him back to earth with a start. "Henry, whatever are you doing to that poor bear? Look at him! He's covered all over with cream and jam."

Mr. Brown jumped up in confusion. "He seemed rather hungry," he answered, lamely.

Mrs. Brown turned to her daughter. "This is what happens when I leave your father alone for five minutes."

Judy clapped her hands excitedly. "Oh, Daddy, is he really going to stay with us?"

"If he does," said Mrs. Brown, "I can see someone other than your father will have to look after him. Just look at the mess he's in!"

Paddington, who all this time had been too interested in his bun to worry about what was going on, suddenly became aware that people were talking about him. He looked up to see that Mrs. Brown had been joined by a little girl, with laughing blue eyes and long, fair hair. He jumped up, meaning to raise his hat, and in his haste slipped on a patch of strawberry

jam which somehow or other had found its way on to
the glass tabletop. For a brief moment he had a dizzy
impression of everything and everyone being upside
down. He waved his paws wildly in the air and then,
before anyone could catch him, he somersaulted
backwards and landed with a splash in his saucer of
tea. He jumped up even quicker than he had sat down,
because the tea was still very hot, and promptly
stepped into Mr. Brown's cup.

Judy threw back her head and laughed until the
tears rolled down her face. "Oh, Mummy, isn't he
funny!" she cried.

Paddington, who didn't think it at all funny, stood
for a moment with one foot on the table and the other
in Mr. Brown's tea. There were large patches of white
cream all over his face, and on his left ear there was a
lump of strawberry jam.

"You wouldn't think," said Mrs. Brown, "that anyone could get in such a state with just one bun."

Mr. Brown coughed. He had just caught the stern eye of a waitress on the other side of the counter. "Perhaps," he said, "we'd better go. I'll see if I can find a taxi." He picked up Judy's belongings and hurried outside.

Paddington stepped gingerly off the table and, with a last look at the sticky remains of his bun, climbed down onto the floor.

Judy took one of his paws. "Come along, Paddington. We'll take you home and you can have a nice hot bath. Then you can tell me all about South America. I'm sure you must have had lots of wonderful adventures."

"I have," said Paddington, earnestly. "Lots. Things are always happening to me. I'm that sort of bear."

When they came out of the buffet Mr. Brown had already found a taxi and he waved them across. The driver looked hard at Paddington and then at the inside of his nice, clean taxi.

"Bears is sixpence extra," he said, gruffly. "Sticky bears is ninepence!"

"He can't help being sticky, driver," said Mr. Brown. "He's just had a nasty accident."

The driver hesitated. "All right, 'op in. But mind none of it comes off on me interior. I only cleaned it out this morning."

The Browns trooped obediently into the back of the taxi. Mr. and Mrs. Brown and Judy sat in the back, while Paddington stood on a tip-up seat behind the driver so that he could see out of the window.

The sun was shining as they drove out of the station and after the gloom and the noise everything seemed bright and cheerful. They swept past a group of people at a bus stop and Paddington waved. Several people stared and one man raised his hat in return. It was all very friendly. After weeks of sitting alone in a lifeboat there was so much to see. There were people and cars and big, red buses everywhere—it wasn't a bit like Darkest Peru.

Paddington kept one eye out of the window in case he missed anything. With his other eye he carefully examined Mr. and Mrs. Brown and Judy. Mr. Brown was fat and jolly, with a big moustache and glasses, while Mrs. Brown, who was also rather plump, looked like a larger edition of Judy. Paddington had just decided he was going to like staying with the Browns when the glass window behind the driver shot back and a gruff voice said, "Where did you say you wanted to go?"

Mr. Brown leaned forward. "Number thirty-two, Windsor Gardens."

The driver cupped his ear with one hand. "Can't 'ear you," he shouted.

Paddington tapped him on the shoulder. "Number thirty-two, Windsor Gardens," he repeated.

The taxi driver jumped at the sound of Paddington's voice and narrowly missed hitting a bus. He looked down at his shoulder and glared. "Cream!" he said, bitterly. "All over me new coat!"

Judy giggled and Mr. and Mrs. Brown exchanged glances. Mr. Brown peered at the meter. He half expected to see a sign go up saying they had to pay another sixpence.

"I beg your pardon," said Paddington. He bent forward and tried to rub the stain off with his other

paw. Several bun crumbs and a smear of jam added
themselves mysteriously to the taxi driver's coat. The
driver gave Paddington a long, hard look. Paddington
raised his hat and the driver slammed the window shut
again.

"Oh dear," said Mrs. Brown. "We really shall have to
give him a bath as soon as we get indoors. It's getting
everywhere."

Paddington looked thoughtful. It wasn't so much
that he didn't like baths; he really didn't mind being
covered with jam and cream. It seemed a pity to wash
it all off quite so soon. But before he had time to
consider the matter the taxi stopped and the Browns
began to climb out. Paddington picked up his suitcase
and followed Judy up a flight of white steps to a big
green door.

"Now you're going to meet Mrs. Bird," said Judy. "She looks after us. She's a bit fierce sometimes and she grumbles a lot but she doesn't really mean it. I'm sure you'll like her."

Paddington felt his knees begin to tremble. He looked around for Mr. and Mrs. Brown, but they appeared to be having some sort of argument with the taxi driver. Behind the door he could hear footsteps approaching.

"I'm sure I shall like her, if you say so," he said, catching sight of his reflection on the brightly polished letter box. "But will she like me?"

As it turns out, Mrs. Bird does take a fancy to Paddington. And, of course, Paddington has a great many funny adventures in London. In addition to *A Bear Called Paddington*, Michael Bond has written other Paddington books, including *Paddington Abroad* and *Paddington at Large*. And if it's real bears you want, you will enjoy *The Mighty Bears* by Robert McClung, which has photographs of all kinds of bears.

J's the Jumping Jay-Walker

by Phyllis McGinley

J's the jumping Jay-walker,
  A sort of human jeep.
He crosses where the lights are red.
  Before he looks, he'll leap!
Then many a wheel
Begins to squeal,
  And many a brake to slam.
He turns your knees to jelly
  And the traffic into jam.

Freddy

by Dennis Lee

Here is the story
Of Freddy, my friend,
Who ran out in the traffic,
And that is the end.

Sing a Song of People

by Lois Lenski

Sing a song of people
  Walking fast or slow;
People in the city,
  Up and down they go.

  People on the sidewalk,
  People on the bus;
  People passing, passing,
  In back and front of us.
  People on the subway
  Underneath the ground;
  People riding taxis
  Round and round and round.

  People with their hats on,
  Going in the doors;
  People with umbrellas
  When it rains and pours.
  People in tall buildings
  And in stores below;
  Riding elevators
  Up and down they go.

  People walking singly,
  People in a crowd;
  People saying nothing,
  People talking loud.
  People laughing, smiling,
  Grumpy people too;
  People who just hurry
  And never look at you!

Sing a song of people
  Who like to come and go;
Sing of city people
  You see but never know!

Sing a Song of Subways

by Eve Merriam

Sing a song of subways,
Never see the sun;
Four-and-twenty people
In room for one.

When the doors are opened—
Everybody run.

252

Song of the Train

by David McCord

Clickety-clack,
Wheels on the track,
This is the way
They begin the attack:
Click-ety-clack,
Click-ety-clack,
Click-ety, *clack*-ety,
Click-ety
Clack.

Clickety-clack,
Over the crack,
Faster and faster
The song of the track:
Clickety-clack,
Clickety-clack,
Clickety, clackety,
Clackety.
Clack.

Riding in front,
Riding in back,
Everyone hears
The song of the track:
Clickety-clack,
Clickety-clack,
Clickety, *clickety*,
Clackety
Clack.

Rudolph Is Tired of the City

by Gwendolyn Brooks

These buildings are too close to me.
I'd like to PUSH away.
I'd like to live in the country,
And spread my arms all day.

I'd like to spread my breath out, too—
As farmers' sons and daughters do.

I'd tend the cows and chickens.
I'd do the other chores.
Then, all the hours left I'd go
A-SPREADING out-of-doors.

Pippi Goes to the Circus

from *Pippi Longstocking* by Astrid Lindgren
translated from the Swedish by Florence Lamborn

Way out at the end of a tiny little town was an old
overgrown garden, and in the garden was an old house,
and in the house lived Pippi Longstocking. She was
nine years old, and she lived there all alone. She had
no mother and no father, and that was of course very
nice because there was no one to tell her to go to bed
just when she was having the most fun, and no one
who could make her take cod-liver oil when she much
preferred caramel candy.

Once upon a time Pippi had had a father of whom
she was extremely fond. Naturally she had had a
mother too, but that was so long ago that Pippi didn't
remember her at all. Her mother had died when Pippi
was just a tiny baby....

Her father Pippi had not forgotten. He was a sea
captain who sailed on the great ocean, and Pippi had
sailed with him in his ship until one day her father
blew overboard in a storm and disappeared. But Pippi

was absolutely certain that he would come back. She would never believe that he had drowned; she was sure he had floated until he landed on an island inhabited by cannibals. And she thought he had become the king of all the cannibals and went around with a golden crown on his head all day long. . . .

Her father had bought the old house in the garden many years ago. He thought he would live there with Pippi when he grew old and couldn't sail the seas any longer. And then this annoying thing had to happen, that he blew into the ocean, and while Pippi was waiting for him to come back she went straight home to Villa Villekulla. That was the name of the house. It stood there ready and waiting for her. One lovely summer evening she had said good-by to all the sailors on her father's boat. They were all so fond of Pippi, and she of them.

"So long, boys," she said and kissed each one on the forehead. "Don't you worry about me. I'll always come out on top."

Two things she took with her from the ship: a little monkey whose name was Mr. Nilsson—he was a present from her father—and a big suitcase full of gold pieces. The sailors stood up on the deck and watched as long as they could see her. She walked straight ahead without looking back at all, with Mr. Nilsson on her shoulder and her suitcase in her hand.

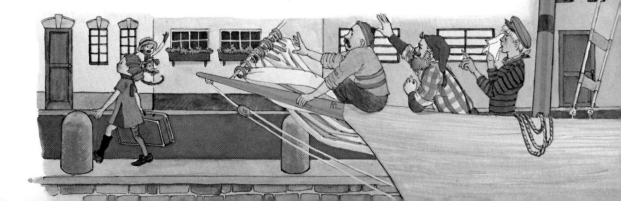

"A remarkable child," said one of the sailors as Pippi disappeared in the distance.

He was right. Pippi was indeed a remarkable child. The most remarkable thing about her was that she was so strong. She was so very strong that in the whole wide world there was not a single police officer who was as strong as she. Why, she could lift a whole horse if she wanted to! And she wanted to. She had a horse of her own that she had bought with one of her many gold pieces the day she came home to Villa Villekulla. She had always longed for a horse, and now here he was living on the porch. When Pippi wanted to drink her afternoon coffee there, she simply lifted him down into the garden.

Beside Villa Villekulla was another garden and another house. In that house lived a father and mother and two charming children, a boy and a girl. The boy's name was Tommy and the girl's Annika. . . .

On that lovely summer evening when Pippi for the first time stepped over the threshold of Villa Villekulla, Tommy and Annika were not at home. They had gone to visit their grandmother for a week; and so they had no idea that anybody had moved into the house next door. On the first day after they came home again they stood by the gate, looking out onto the street, and even then they didn't know that there actually was a playmate so near. Just as they were standing there considering what they could do and wondering whether anything exciting was likely to happen or whether it was going to be one of those dull days when they couldn't think of anything to play—just then the gate of Villa Villekulla opened and a little girl stepped out. She was the most remarkable

girl Tommy and Annika had ever seen. She was Miss
Pippi Longstocking out for her morning promenade.
This is the way she looked:

Her hair, the color of a carrot, was braided in two
tight braids that stuck straight out. Her nose was the
shape of a very small potato and was dotted all over
with freckles. It must be admitted that the mouth
under this nose was a very wide one, with strong white
teeth. Her dress was rather unusual. Pippi herself had
made it. She had meant it to be blue, but there wasn't
quite enough blue cloth, so Pippi had sewed little red
pieces on it here and there. On her long thin legs she
wore a pair of long stockings, one brown and the other
black; and she had on a pair of black shoes that were
exactly twice as long as her feet. These shoes her
father had bought for her in South America so that
Pippi should have something to grow into, and she
never wanted to wear any others.

But the thing that made Tommy and Annika open

their eyes widest of all was the monkey sitting on the strange girl's shoulder. It was a little monkey, dressed in blue pants, yellow jacket, and a white straw hat.

Pippi walked along the street with one foot on the sidewalk and the other in the gutter. Tommy and Annika watched as long as they could see her. In a little while she came back, and now she was walking backward. That was because she didn't want to turn around to get home. When she reached Tommy's and Annika's gate she stopped.

The children looked at each other in silence. At last Tommy spoke. "Why did you walk backward?"

"Why did I walk backward?" said Pippi. "Isn't this a free country? Can't a person walk any way he wants to? For that matter, let me tell you that in Egypt everybody walks that way, and nobody thinks it's the least bit strange."

"How do you know?" asked Tommy. "You've never been in Egypt, have you?"

"I've never been in Egypt? Indeed I have. That's one thing you can be sure of. I have been all over the world and seen many things stranger than people walking backward. I wonder what you would have said if I had come along walking on my hands the way they do in Farthest India."

"Now you must be lying," said Tommy.

Pippi thought a moment. "You're right," she said sadly, "I am lying."

"It's wicked to lie," said Annika, who had at last gathered up enough courage to speak.

"Yes, it's very wicked to lie," said Pippi even more sadly. "But I forget it now and then. And how can you expect a little child whose mother is an angel and whose father is king of a cannibal island and who herself has sailed on the ocean all her life—how can you expect her to tell the truth always? And for that matter," she continued, her whole freckled face lighting up, "let me tell you that in the Belgian Congo there is not a single person who tells the truth. They lie all day long. Begin at seven in the morning and keep on until sundown. So if I should happen to lie now and then, you must try to excuse me and to remember that it is only because I stayed in the Belgian Congo a little too long. We can be friends anyway, can't we?"

"Oh, sure," said Tommy and realized suddenly that this was not going to be one of those dull days.

"By the way, why couldn't you come and have breakfast with me?" asked Pippi.

"Why not?" said Tommy. "Come on, let's go."

"Oh, yes, let's," said Annika.

"But first I must introduce you to Mr. Nilsson," said
Pippi, and the little monkey took off his cap and
bowed politely.

Then they all went in through Villa Villekulla's
tumbledown garden gate, along the gravel path,
bordered with old moss-covered trees—really good
climbing trees they seemed to be—up to the house, and
on to the porch. There stood the horse, munching oats
out of a soup bowl.

"Why do you have a horse on the porch?" asked
Tommy. All horses he knew lived in stables.

"Well," said Pippi thoughtfully, "he'd be in the way
in the kitchen, and he doesn't like the parlor."

Tommy and Annika patted the horse and then went
on into the house. It had a kitchen, a parlor, and a
bedroom. But it certainly looked as if Pippi had
forgotten to do her Friday cleaning that week. Tommy
and Annika looked around cautiously just in case the
King of the Cannibal Isles might be sitting in a corner

somewhere. They had never seen a cannibal king in all
their lives. But there was no father to be seen, nor any
mother either.

Annika said anxiously, "Do you live here all alone?"

"Of course not!" said Pippi. "Mr. Nilsson and the
horse live here too."

"Yes, but I mean, don't you have any mother or
father here?"

"No, not the least little tiny bit of a one," said Pippi
happily.

"But who tells you when to go to bed at night and
things like that?" asked Annika.

"I tell myself," said Pippi. "First I tell myself in a
nice friendly way; and then, if I don't mind, I tell
myself again more sharply; and if I still don't mind,
then I'm in for a spanking—see?"

Tommy and Annika didn't see at all but they thought maybe it was a good way. Meanwhile they had come out into the kitchen.... Pippi took three eggs and threw them up in the air. One fell down on her head and broke so that the yolk ran into her eyes, but the others she caught skillfully in a bowl, where they smashed to pieces.

"I always did hear that egg yolk was good for the hair," said Pippi, wiping her eyes. "You wait and see—mine will soon begin to grow so fast it crackles...."

While she was speaking Pippi had neatly picked the eggshells out of the bowl with her fingers. Now she took a bath brush that hung on the wall and began to beat the pancake batter so hard that it splashed all over the walls. At last she poured what was left onto a griddle that stood on the stove.

When the pancake was brown on one side she tossed it halfway up to the ceiling, so that it turned right around in the air, and then she caught it on the griddle again. And when it was ready she threw it straight across the kitchen right onto a plate that stood on the table.

"Eat!" she cried. "Eat before it gets cold!"

And Tommy and Annika ate and thought it a very good pancake.

Afterward Pippi invited them to step into the parlor. There was only one piece of furniture in there. It was a huge chest with many tiny drawers. Pippi opened the drawers and showed Tommy and Annika all the treasures she kept there. There were wonderful birds' eggs, strange shells and stones, pretty little boxes, lovely silver mirrors, pearl necklaces, and many other things that Pippi and her father had bought on their journeys around the world. . . .

"Suppose you go home now," said Pippi, "so that you can come back tomorrow. Because if you don't go home you can't come back, and that would be a shame."

Tommy and Annika agreed that it would indeed. So they went home—past the horse, who had now eaten up all the oats, and out through the gate of Villa Villekulla. Mr. Nilsson waved his hat at them as they left.

Annika woke up early the next morning. She jumped out of bed and ran over to Tommy.

"Wake up, Tommy," she cried, pulling him by the

arm, "wake up and let's go and see that funny girl with the big shoes."

Tommy was wide awake in an instant.

"I knew, even while I was sleeping, that something exciting was going to happen today, but I didn't remember what it was," he said as he yanked off his pajama jacket. Off they went to the bathroom; washed themselves and brushed their teeth much faster than usual; had their clothes on in a twinkling; and a whole hour before their mother expected them came sliding down the banister and landed at the breakfast table. Down they sat and announced that they wanted their hot chocolate right off that very moment. . . .

A circus had come to the little town, and all the children were begging their mothers and fathers for permission to go. Of course Tommy and Annika asked to go too, and their kind father immediately gave them some money.

Clutching it tightly in their hands, they rushed over to Pippi's. She was on the porch with her horse, braiding his tail into tiny pigtails and tying each one with red ribbon.

"I think it's his birthday today," she announced, "so he has to be all dressed up."

"Pippi," said Tommy, all out of breath because they had been running so fast, "Pippi, do you want to go with us to the circus?"

"I can go with you most anywhere," answered Pippi, "but whether I can go to the surkus or not I don't know, because I don't know what a surkus is. Does it hurt?"

"Silly!" said Tommy, "of course it doesn't hurt; it's fun. Horses and clowns and pretty ladies that walk the tightrope."

"But it costs money," said Annika, opening her small fist to see if the shiny half dollar and the quarters were still there.

"I'm rich as a troll," said Pippi, "so I guess I can buy a surkus all right. But it'll be crowded here if I have more horses. The clowns and the pretty ladies I could keep in the laundry, but it's harder to know what to do with the horses."

"Oh, don't be silly," said Tommy, "you don't buy a circus. It costs money to go and look at it—see?"

"Preserve us!" cried Pippi and shut her eyes tightly. "It costs money to look? And here I go around goggling all day long. Goodness knows how much money I've goggled up already!"

Then, little by little, she opened one eye very carefully, and it rolled round and round in her head. "Cost what it may," she said, "I must take a look!"

At last Tommy and Annika managed to explain to Pippi what a circus really was, and she took some gold pieces out of her suitcase. Then she put on her hat, which was as big as a millstone, and off they all went.

There were crowds of people outside the circus tent and a long line at the ticket window. But at last it was Pippi's turn. She stuck her head through the window and stared at the dear old lady sitting there.

"How much does it cost to look at you?" Pippi asked.

But the old lady was a foreigner who did not understand what Pippi meant and answered in broken Swedish.

"Little girl, it costs a dollar and a quarter in the grandstand and seventy-five cents on the benches and twenty-five cents for standing room."

Now Tommy interrupted and said that Pippi wanted

a seventy-five-cent ticket. Pippi put down a gold piece
and the old lady looked suspiciously at it. She bit it too,
to see if it was genuine. At last she was convinced that
it really was gold and gave Pippi her ticket and a
great deal of change in silver.

"What would I do with all those nasty little white
coins?" asked Pippi disgustedly. "Keep them and then
I can look at you twice. In the standing room."

As Pippi absolutely refused to accept any change,
the lady changed her ticket for one for the grandstand
and gave Tommy and Annika grandstand tickets too
without their having to pay a single penny. In that
way Pippi, Tommy, and Annika came to sit on some
beautiful red chairs right next to the ring. Tommy and
Annika turned around several times to wave to their
schoolmates, who were sitting much farther away.

"This is a remarkable place," said Pippi, looking

around in astonishment. "But, see, they've spilled sawdust all over the floor! Not that I'm overfussy myself, but that does look careless to me."

Tommy explained that all circuses had sawdust on the floor for the horses to run around in.

On a platform nearby the circus band suddenly began to play a thundering march. Pippi clapped her hands wildly and jumped up and down with delight.

"Does it cost money to hear too?" she asked, "or can you do that for nothing?"

At that moment the curtain in front of the performers' entrance was drawn aside, and the ringmaster in a black frock coat, with a whip in his hand, came running in, followed by ten white horses with red plumes on their heads.

The ringmaster cracked his whip, and all the horses galloped around the ring. Then he cracked it again, and all the horses stood still with their front feet up on the railing around the ring.

One of them had stopped directly in front of the children. Annika didn't like to have a horse so near her

and drew back in her chair as far as she could, but Pippi leaned forward and took the horse's right foot in her hands.

"Hello, there," she said, "my horse sent you his best wishes. It's his birthday today too, but he has bows on his tail instead of on his head."

Luckily she dropped the foot before the ringmaster cracked his whip again, because then all the horses jumped away from the railing and began to run around the ring.

When the number was over, the ringmaster bowed politely and the horses ran out. In an instant the curtain opened again for a coal-black horse. On its back stood a beautiful lady dressed in green silk tights. The program said her name was Miss Carmencita.

The horse trotted around in the sawdust, and Miss Carmencita stood calmly on his back and smiled. But then something happened; just as the horse passed Pippi's seat, something came swishing through the air—and it was none other than Pippi herself. And there she stood on the horse's back, behind Miss Carmencita. At first Miss Carmencita was so astonished that she nearly fell off the horse. Then she got mad. She began to strike out with her hands behind her back to make Pippi jump off. But that didn't work.

"Take it easy," said Pippi. "Do you think you're the only one who can have any fun? Other people have paid too, haven't they?"

Then Miss Carmencita tried to jump off herself, but that didn't work either, because Pippi was holding her tightly around the waist. At that the audience couldn't

help laughing. They thought it was so funny to see the lovely Miss Carmencita held against her will by a little redheaded youngster who stood there on the horse's back in her enormous shoes and looked as if she had never done anything except perform in a circus.

But the ringmaster didn't laugh. He turned toward an attendant in a red uniform and made a sign to him to go and stop the horse.

"Is this number already over," asked Pippi in a disappointed tone, "just when we were having so much fun?"

"Horrible child!" hissed the ringmaster between his teeth. "Get out of here!"

Pippi looked at him sadly. "Why are you mad at me?" she asked. "What's the matter? I thought we were here to have fun."

She skipped off the horse and went back to her seat. But now two huge guards came to throw her out. They took hold of her and tried to lift her up.

They couldn't do it. Pippi sat absolutely still, and it was impossible to budge her although they tried as hard as they could. At last they shrugged their shoulders and went off....

The next number was about to begin.... The ringmaster ... bowed to the audience, and said, "Ladies and gentlemen, in a moment you will be privileged to see the Greatest Marvel of all time, the Strongest Man in the World, the Mighty Adolf, whom no one has yet been able to conquer. Here he comes, ladies and gentlemen. Allow me to present to you THE MIGHTY ADOLF."

And into the ring stepped a man who looked as big as a giant. He wore flesh-colored tights and had a leopard skin draped around his stomach. He bowed to the audience and looked very pleased with himself.

"Look at these muscles," said the ringmaster and squeezed the Mighty Adolf's arm where the muscles stood out like balls under the skin.

"And now, ladies and gentlemen, I have a very special invitation for you. Who will challenge the Mighty Adolf in a wrestling match? Who of you dares to try his strength against the World's Strongest Man? A hundred dollars for anyone who can conquer the Mighty Adolf! A hundred dollars, ladies and gentlemen! Think of that! Who will be the first to try?"

Nobody came forth.

"What did he say?" said Pippi.

"He says that anybody who can lick that big man will get a hundred dollars," answered Tommy.

"I can," said Pippi, "but I think it's too bad to, because he looks nice."

"Oh, no, you couldn't," said Annika, "he's the strongest man in the world."

"*Man*, yes," said Pippi, "but I am the strongest girl in the world, remember that."

Meanwhile the Mighty Adolf was lifting heavy iron weights and bending thick iron rods in the middle just to show how strong he was.

"Oh, come now, ladies and gentlemen," cried the ringmaster, "is there really nobody here who wants to earn a hundred dollars? Shall I really be forced to keep this myself?" And he waved a bill in the air.

"No, that you certainly won't be forced to do," said Pippi and stepped over the railing into the ring.

The ringmaster was absolutely wild when he saw her. "Get out of here! I don't want to see any more of you," he hissed.

"Why do you always have to be so unfriendly?" said Pippi reproachfully. "I just want to fight with Mighty Adolf."

"This is no place for jokes," said the ringmaster. "Get out of here before the Mighty Adolf hears your impudent nonsense."

But Pippi went right by the ringmaster and up to Mighty Adolf. She took his hand and shook it heartily.

"Shall we fight a little, you and I?" she asked.

Mighty Adolf looked at her but didn't understand a word.

"In one minute I'll begin," said Pippi.

And begin she did. She grabbed Mighty Adolf around the waist, and before anyone knew what was happening she had thrown him on the mat. Mighty Adolf leaped up, his face absolutely scarlet.

"Atta girl, Pippi!" shrieked Tommy and Annika, so loudly that all the people at the circus heard it and began to shriek "Atta girl, Pippi!" too. The ringmaster sat on the railing, wringing his hands. He was mad, but Mighty Adolf was madder. Never in his life had he

experienced anything so humiliating as this. And he
certainly intended to show that redheaded girl what
kind of a man Mighty Adolf really was. He rushed at
Pippi and caught her around the waist, but Pippi stood
firm as a rock.

"You can do better than that," she said to encourage
him. Then she wriggled out of his grasp, and in the
twinkling of an eye Mighty Adolf was on the mat again.
Pippi stood beside him, waiting. She didn't have to
wait long. With a roar he was up again, rushing at her.

"Tiddelipom and piddeliday," said Pippi.

All the people in the tent stamped their feet and
threw their hats in the air and shouted, "Hurrah,
Pippi!"

When Mighty Adolf came rushing at her for the third
time, Pippi lifted him high in the air and, with her arms
straight above her, carried him clear around the ring. Then
she laid him down on the mat again and held him there.

"Now, little fellow," said she, "I don't think we'll bother about this any more. We'll never have any more fun than we've had already."

"Pippi is the winner! Pippi is the winner!" cried all the people.

Mighty Adolf stole out as fast as he could, and the ringmaster had to go up and hand Pippi the hundred dollars, although he looked as if he'd much prefer to eat her.

"Here you are, young lady, here you are," said he. "One hundred dollars."

"That thing!" said Pippi scornfully. "What would I want with that old piece of paper. Take it and use it to fry herring on if you want to." And she went back to her seat.

"This is certainly a long surkus," she said to Tommy and Annika. "I think I'll take a little snooze, but wake me if they need my help about anything else."

And then she lay back in her chair and went to sleep at once. There she lay and snored while the clowns, the sword swallowers, and the snake charmers did their tricks for Tommy and Annika and all the rest of the people at the circus.

"Just the same, I think Pippi was best of all," whispered Tommy to Annika.

As you have discovered, Pippi is a very unusual girl. In *Pippi Longstocking*, the book from which this story came, you can join this supergirl as she entertains two burglars, upsets a school classroom, and has many more hilarious adventures. And by then, you will also want to read *Pippi Goes on Board* and *Pippi in the South Seas*.

Mummy Slept Late and Daddy Fixed Breakfast
by John Ciardi

Daddy fixed the breakfast.
He made us each a waffle.
It looked like gravel pudding.
It tasted something awful.

"Ha, ha," he said, "I'll try again.
This time I'll get it right."
But what *I* got was in between
Bituminous and anthracite.

"A little too well done? Oh well,
I'll have to start all over."
That time what landed on my plate
Looked like a manhole cover.

I tried to cut it with a fork:
The fork gave off a spark.
I tried a knife and twisted it
Into a question mark.

I tried it with a hack-saw.
I tried it with a torch.
It didn't even make a dent.
It didn't even scorch.

The next time Dad gets breakfast
When Mommy's sleeping late,
I think I'll skip the waffles.
I'd sooner eat the plate!

Daddy Fell into the Pond

by Alfred Noyes

Everyone grumbled. The sky was gray.
We had nothing to do and nothing to say.
We were nearing the end of a dismal day,
And there seemed to be nothing beyond,
   THEN
    Daddy fell into the pond!

And everyone's face grew merry and bright,
And Timothy danced for sheer delight.
"Give me the camera, quick, oh quick!
He's crawling out of the duckweed." *Click!*

Then the gardener suddenly slapped his knee,
And doubled up, shaking silently,
And the ducks all quacked as if they were daft
And it sounded as if the old drake laughed.
O, there wasn't a thing that didn't respond
   WHEN
    Daddy fell into the pond!

Christmas
in the Little House

from *Little House in the Big Woods*
by Laura Ingalls Wilder
pictures by Garth Williams

More than a hundred years ago, a little girl named
Laura lived in a log house at the edge of a great
forest in Wisconsin. She lived with her parents, two
sisters, a bulldog named Jack, and a cat named Black
Susan. The woods were filled with wild animals. The
nearest people lived almost a day's journey away. This
is a true story of the author's own childhood.

⚜ ⚜ ⚜

Christmas was coming.

The little log house was almost buried in snow. Great
drifts were banked against the walls and windows, and
in the morning when Pa opened the door, there was a
wall of snow as high as Laura's head. Pa took the
shovel and shoveled it away, and then he shoveled a
path to the barn, where the horses and the cows were
snug and warm in their stalls.

The days were clear and bright. Laura and Mary
stood on chairs by the window and looked out across

276

the glittering snow at the glittering trees. Snow was piled all along their bare, dark branches, and it sparkled in the sunshine. Icicles hung from the eaves of the house to the snowbanks, great icicles as large at the top as Laura's arm. They were like glass and full of sharp lights.

Pa's breath hung in the air like smoke, when he came along the path from the barn. He breathed it out in clouds and it froze in white frost on his mustache and beard.

When he came in, stamping the snow from his boots, and caught Laura up in a bear's hug against his cold, big coat, his mustache was beaded with little drops of melting frost.

Every night he was busy, working on a large piece of board and two small pieces. He whittled them with his knife, he rubbed them with sandpaper and with the palm of his hand, until when Laura touched them they felt soft and smooth as silk.

Then with his sharp jackknife he worked at them, cutting the edges of the large one into little peaks and towers, with a large star carved on the very tallest point. He cut little holes through the wood. He cut the holes in shapes of windows, and little stars, and crescent moons, and circles. All around them he carved tiny leaves, and flowers, and birds.

One of the little boards he shaped in a lovely curve, and around its edges he carved leaves and flowers and stars, and through it he cut crescent moons and curlicues.

Around the edges of the smallest board he carved a tiny flowering vine.

He made the tiniest shavings, cutting very slowly

and carefully, making whatever he thought would be pretty.

At last he had the pieces finished and one night he fitted them together. When this was done, the large piece was a beautifully carved back for a smooth little shelf across its middle. The large star was at the very top of it. The curved piece supported the shelf underneath, and it was carved beautifully, too. And the little vine ran around the edge of the shelf.

Pa had made this bracket for a Christmas present for Ma. He hung it carefully against the log wall between the windows, and Ma stood her little china woman on the shelf.

The little china woman had a china bonnet on her head, and china curls hung around her china neck. Her china dress was laced across in front, and she wore a pale-pink china apron and little gilt china shoes. She was beautiful, standing on the shelf with flowers and leaves and birds and moons carved all around her, and the large star at the very top.

Ma was busy all day long, cooking good things for Christmas. She baked salt-rising bread and rye'n'Injun bread, and Swedish crackers, and a huge pan of baked beans, with salt pork and molasses. She baked vinegar pies and dried-apple pies, and filled a big jar with cookies, and she let Laura and Mary lick the cake spoon.

One morning she boiled molasses and sugar together until they made a thick syrup, and Pa brought in two pans of clean, white snow from outdoors. Laura and Mary each had a pan, and Pa and Ma showed them how to pour the dark syrup in little streams on to the snow.

They made circles, and curlicues, and squiggledy things, and these hardened at once and were candy. Laura and Mary might eat one piece each, but the rest was saved for Christmas Day.

All this was done because Aunt Eliza and Uncle Peter and the cousins, Peter and Alice and Ella, were coming to spend Christmas.

The day before Christmas they came. Laura and Mary heard the gay ringing of sleigh bells, growing louder every moment, and then the big bobsled[1] came out of the woods and drove up to the gate. Aunt Eliza and Uncle Peter and the cousins were in it, all covered up, under blankets and robes and buffalo skins.

They were wrapped up in so many coats and mufflers and veils and shawls that they looked like big, shapeless bundles.

When they all came in, the little house was full and running over. Black Susan ran out and hid in the barn, but Jack leaped in circles through the snow, barking as

---

1. A bobsled was a big sled or sleigh pulled by horses.
   Sometimes it had two pairs of runners.

though he would never stop. Now there were cousins to play with!

As soon as Aunt Eliza had unwrapped them, Peter and Alice and Ella and Laura and Mary began to run and shout. At last Aunt Eliza told them to be quiet. Then Alice said:

"I'll tell you what let's do. Let's make pictures."

Alice said they must go outdoors to do it, and Ma thought it was too cold for Laura to play outdoors. But when she saw how disappointed Laura was, she said she might go, after all, for a little while. She put on Laura's coat and mittens and the warm cape with the hood, and wrapped a muffler around her neck, and let her go.

Laura had never had so much fun. All morning she

played outdoors in the snow with Alice and Ella and Peter and Mary, making pictures. The way they did it was this:

Each one climbed up on a stump, and then all at once, holding their arms out wide, they fell off the stumps into the soft, deep snow. They fell flat on their faces. Then they tried to get up without spoiling the marks they made when they fell. If they did it well, there in the snow were five holes, shaped almost exactly like four little girls and a boy, arms and legs and all. They called these their pictures.

They played so hard all day that when night came they were too excited to sleep. But they must sleep, or Santa Claus would not come. So they hung their stockings by the fireplace, and said their prayers, and went to bed—Alice and Ella and Mary and Laura all in one big bed on the floor.

Peter had the trundle bed.[2] Aunt Eliza and Uncle Peter were going to sleep in the big bed, and another bed was made on the attic floor for Pa and Ma. The buffalo robes and all the blankets had been brought in from Uncle Peter's sled, so there were enough covers for everybody.

Pa and Ma and Aunt Eliza and Uncle Peter sat by the fire, talking. And just as Laura was drifting off to sleep, she heard Uncle Peter say:

"Eliza had a narrow squeak the other day, when I was away at Lake City. You know Prince, that big dog of mine?"

Laura was wide awake at once. She always liked to

---

2. A trundle bed is a low bed. When not in use, it can be pushed under a regular bed.

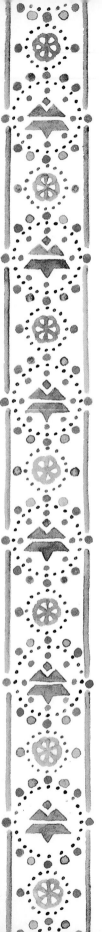

hear about dogs. She lay still as a mouse, and looked at
the firelight flickering on the log walls, and listened to
Uncle Peter.

"Well," Uncle Peter said, "early in the morning Eliza
started to the spring to get a pail of water, and Prince
was following her. She got to the edge of the ravine,
where the path goes down to the spring, and all of a
sudden Prince set his teeth in the back of her skirt
and pulled.

"You know what a big dog he is. Eliza scolded him,
but he wouldn't let go, and he's so big and strong she
couldn't get away from him. He kept backing and
pulling, till he tore a piece out of her skirt."

"It was my blue print," Aunt Eliza said to Ma.

"Dear me!" Ma said.

"He tore a big piece right out of the back of it,"
Aunt Eliza said. "I was so mad I could have whipped
him for it. But he growled at me."

"Prince growled at you?" Pa said.

"Yes," said Aunt Eliza.

"So then she started on again toward the spring,"
Uncle Peter went on. "But Prince jumped into the path
ahead of her and snarled at her. He paid no attention
to her talking and scolding. He just kept on showing
his teeth and snarling, and when she tried to get past

282

him he kept in front of her and snapped at her. That scared her."

"I should think it would!" Ma said.

"He was so savage, I thought he was going to bite me," said Aunt Eliza. "I believe he would have."

"I never heard of such a thing!" said Ma. "What on earth did you do?"

"I turned right around and ran into the house where the children were, and slammed the door," Aunt Eliza answered.

"Of course Prince was savage with strangers," said Uncle Peter. "But he was always so kind to Eliza and the children I felt perfectly safe to leave them with him. Eliza couldn't understand it at all.

"After she got into the house he kept pacing around it and growling. Every time she started to open the door he jumped at her and snarled."

"Had he gone mad?" said Ma.

"That's what I thought," Aunt Eliza said. "I didn't know what to do. There I was, shut up in the house with the children, and not daring to go out. And we didn't have any water. I couldn't even get any snow to melt. Every time I opened the door so much as a crack, Prince acted like he would tear me to pieces."

"How long did this go on?" Pa asked.

"All day, till late in the afternoon," Aunt Eliza said. "Peter had taken the gun, or I would have shot him."

"Along late in the afternoon," Uncle Peter said, "he got quiet, and lay down in front of the door. Eliza thought he was asleep, and she made up her mind to try to slip past him and get to the spring for some water.

"So she opened the door very quietly, but of course

283

he woke up right away. When he saw she had the
water pail in her hand, he got up and walked ahead of
her to the spring, just the same as usual. And there, all
around the spring in the snow, were the fresh tracks
of a panther[3]."

"The tracks were as big as my hand," said Aunt Eliza.

"Yes," Uncle Peter said, "he was a big fellow. His
tracks were the biggest I ever saw. He would have got
Eliza sure, if Prince had let her go to the spring in the
morning. I saw the tracks. He had been lying up in
that big oak over the spring, waiting for some animal
to come there for water. Undoubtedly he would have
dropped down on her.

"Night was coming on, when she saw the tracks, and
she didn't waste any time getting back to the house
with her pail of water. Prince followed close behind
her, looking back into the ravine now and then."

"I took him into the house with me," Aunt Eliza
said, "and we all stayed inside, till Peter came home."

"Did you get him?" Pa asked Uncle Peter.

"No," Uncle Peter said. "I took my gun and hunted
all round the place, but I couldn't find him. I saw some
more of his tracks. He'd gone on north, farther into
the Big Woods."

Alice and Ella and Mary were all wide awake now,
and Laura put her head under the covers and
whispered to Alice, "My! weren't you scared?"

Alice whispered back that she was scared, but Ella
was scareder. And Ella whispered that she wasn't,
either, any such thing.

---

3. Panther is one name for the animal that is also called a
   mountain lion, a cougar, a catamount, or a puma.

"Well, anyway, you made more fuss about being thirsty," Alice whispered.

They lay there whispering about it till Ma said: "Charles, those children never will get to sleep unless you play for them." So Pa got his fiddle.

The room was still and warm and full of firelight. Ma's shadow, and Aunt Eliza's and Uncle Peter's were big and quivering on the walls in the flickering firelight, and Pa's fiddle sang merrily to itself.

It sang "Money Musk," and "The Red Heifer," "The Devil's Dream," and "Arkansas Traveler." And Laura went to sleep while Pa and the fiddle were both softly singing:

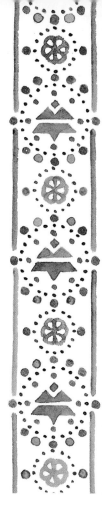

"My darling Nelly Gray, they have taken you away,
And I'll never see my darling any more. . . ."

In the morning they all woke up almost at the same moment. They looked at their stockings, and something was in them. Santa Claus had been there. Alice and Ella and Laura in their red flannel nightgowns and Peter in his red flannel nightshirt, all ran shouting to see what he had brought.

In each stocking there was a pair of bright-red mittens, and there was a long, flat stick of red-and-white-striped peppermint candy, all beautifully notched along each side.

They were all so happy they could hardly speak at first. They just looked with shining eyes at those lovely Christmas presents. But Laura was happiest of all. Laura had a rag doll.

She was a beautiful doll. She had a face of white cloth with black button eyes. A black pencil had made her eyebrows, and her cheeks and her mouth were red

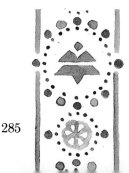

with the ink made from pokeberries.[4] Her hair was black yarn that had been knit and raveled, so that it was curly.

She had little red flannel stockings and little black cloth gaiters for shoes, and her dress was pretty pink and blue calico.

She was so beautiful that Laura could not say a

---

4. Pokeberries are the deep purple berries that grow on the pokeweed plant. They are sometimes called inkberries.

word. She just held her tight and forgot everything else. She did not know that everyone was looking at her, till Aunt Eliza said:

"Did you ever see such big eyes!"

The other girls were not jealous because Laura had mittens, and candy, *and* a doll, because Laura was the littlest girl, except Baby Carrie and Aunt Eliza's little baby, Dolly Varden. The babies were too small for dolls. They were so small they did not even know about Santa Claus. They just put their fingers in their mouths and wriggled because of all the excitement.

Laura sat down on the edge of the bed and held her doll. She loved her red mittens and she loved the candy, but she loved her doll best of all. She named her Charlotte.

Then they all looked at each others' mittens, and tried on their own, and Peter bit a large piece out of his stick of candy, but Alice and Ella and Mary and Laura licked theirs, to make it last longer.

"Well, well!" Uncle Peter said. "Isn't there even one stocking with nothing but a switch in it? My, my, have you all been such good children?"

But they didn't believe that Santa Claus could, really, have given any of them nothing but a switch. That happened to some children, but it couldn't happen to them. It was so hard to be good all the time, every day, for a whole year.

"You mustn't tease the children, Peter," Aunt Eliza said.

Ma said, "Laura, aren't you going to let the other girls hold your doll?" She meant, "Little girls must not be so selfish."

So Laura let Mary take the beautiful doll, and then

Alice held her a minute, and then Ella. They smoothed the pretty dress and admired the red flannel stockings and the gaiters, and the curly woolen hair. But Laura was glad when at last Charlotte was safe in her arms again.

Pa and Uncle Peter had each a pair of new, warm mittens, knit in little squares of red and white. Ma and Aunt Eliza had made them.

Aunt Eliza had brought Ma a large red apple stuck full of cloves. How good it smelled! And it would not spoil, for so many cloves would keep it sound and sweet.

Ma gave Aunt Eliza a little needle-book she had made, with bits of silk for covers and soft white flannel leaves into which to stick the needles. The flannel would keep the needles from rusting.

They all admired Ma's beautiful bracket, and Aunt Eliza said that Uncle Peter had made one for her—of course, with different carving.

Santa Claus had not given them anything at all. Santa Claus did not give grown people presents, but that was not because they had not been good. Pa and Ma were good. It was because they were grown up, and grown people must give each other presents.

Then all the presents must be laid away for a little while. Peter went out with Pa and Uncle Peter to do the chores, and Alice and Ella helped Aunt Eliza make the beds, and Laura and Mary set the table, while Ma got breakfast.

For breakfast there were pancakes, and Ma made a pancake man for each one of the children. Ma called each one in turn to bring their plate, and each could stand by the stove and watch, while with the spoonful of batter Ma put on the arms and the legs and the head. It was exciting to watch her turn the whole little man over, quickly and carefully, on a hot griddle. When it was done, she put it smoking hot on the plate.

Peter ate the head off his man, right away. But Alice and Ella and Mary and Laura ate theirs slowly in little bits, first the arms and legs and then the middle, saving the head for the last.

Today the weather was so cold that they could not play outdoors, but there were the new mittens to admire, and the candy to lick. And they all sat on the floor together and looked at the pictures in the Bible, and the pictures of all kinds of animals and birds in Pa's big green book. Laura kept Charlotte in her arms the whole time.

Then there was the Christmas dinner. Alice and Ella and Peter and Mary and Laura did not say a word at table, for they knew that children should be seen and not heard. But they did not need to ask for second helpings. Ma and Aunt Eliza kept their plates full and let them eat all the good things they could hold.

"Christmas comes but once a year," said Aunt Eliza.

Dinner was early, because Aunt Eliza, Uncle Peter and the cousins had such a long way to go.

"Best the horses can do," Uncle Peter said, "we'll hardly make it home before dark."

So as soon as they had eaten dinner, Uncle Peter and Pa went to put the horses to the sled, while Ma and Aunt Eliza wrapped up the cousins.

They pulled heavy woolen stockings over the woolen stockings and the shoes they were already wearing. They put on mittens and coats and warm hoods and shawls, and wrapped mufflers around their necks and

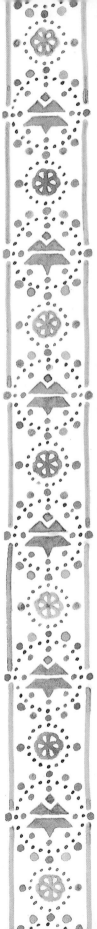

thick woolen veils over their faces. Ma slipped piping
hot baked potatoes into their pockets to keep their
fingers warm, and Aunt Eliza's flatirons were hot on
the stove, ready to put on their feet in the sled. The
blankets and the quilts and the buffalo robes were
warmed, too.

So they all got into the big bobsled, cosy and warm,
and Pa tucked the last robe well in around them.

"Good-by! Good-by!" they called, and off they went,
the horses trotting gaily and the sleigh bells ringing.

In just a little while the merry sound of the bells
was gone, and Christmas was over. But what a happy
Christmas it had been!

If you enjoyed this story, you will want to read the rest
of the book from which it came, *Little House in the Big
Woods*, as well as the other eight books in the "Little
House" series.

June!
by Aileen Fisher

The day is warm
and a breeze is blowing,
the sky is blue
and its eye is glowing,
and everything's new
and green and growing...

My shoes are off
and my socks are showing...

My socks are off...

Do you know how I'm going?
　　　　BAREFOOT!

as my eyes
search
the prairie
I feel the summer
in the spring
　　　a Chippewa Indian song

The Sun Is Stuck
by Myra Cohn Livingston

The sun is stuck.
I mean, it won't move.
I mean it's hot, man, and we need a red-hot poker to
　　pry it loose,
Give it a good shove and roll it across the sky
And make it go down
So we can be cool,
Man.

Something Told
the Wild Geese
by Rachel Field

Something told the wild geese
   It was time to go.
Though the fields lay golden
   Something whispered—"Snow."
Leaves were green and stirring,
   Berries, luster-glossed,
But beneath warm feathers
   Something cautioned—"Frost."
All the sagging orchards
   Steamed with amber spice,
But each wild breast stiffened
   At remembered ice.
Something told the wild geese
   It was time to fly—
Summer sun was on their wings,
   Winter in their cry.

Autumn
by Emily Dickinson

The morns are meeker than they were,
   The nuts are getting brown;
The berry's cheek is plumper,
   The rose is out of town.

The maple wears a gayer scarf,
   The field a scarlet gown.
Lest I should be old-fashioned,
   I'll put a trinket on.

End-of-Summer Poem
by Rowena Bastin Bennett

The little songs of summer are all gone today.
The little insect instruments are all packed away:
The bumblebee's snare drum, the grasshopper's guitar,
The katydid's castanets—I wonder where they are.
The bullfrog's banjo, the cricket's violin,
The dragonfly's cello have ceased their merry din.
Oh, where is the orchestra? From harpist down to drummer
They've all disappeared with the passing of the summer.

Daylight-Saving Time
by Phyllis McGinley

In Spring when maple buds are red,
We turn the Clock an hour ahead;
Which means, each April that arrives,
We lose an hour
Out of our lives.

Who cares? When Autumn birds in flocks
Fly southward, back we turn the Clocks,
And so regain a lovely thing—
That missing hour
We lost last Spring.

Stopping by Woods
on a Snowy Evening
by Robert Frost

Whose woods these are I think I know.
His house is in the village though;
He will not see me stopping here
To watch his woods fill up with snow.

My little horse must think it queer
To stop without a farmhouse near
Between the woods and frozen lake
The darkest evening of the year.

He gives his harness bells a shake
To ask if there is some mistake.
The only other sound's the sweep
Of easy wind and downy flake.

The woods are lovely, dark and deep,
But I have promises to keep,
And miles to go before I sleep.
And miles to go before I sleep.

First Snow
by Marie Louise Allen

Snow makes whiteness where it falls.
The bushes look like popcorn-balls.
And places where I always play,
Look like somewhere else today.

They've All Gone South
by Mary Britton Miller

Redbird, bluebird,
Bird with yellow mouth
All the pretty little birds
Have flown away south,
But the little dusty sparrow
With his wings of rusty brown
For some peculiar reason
Lingers in the town
And little city children
Who wouldn't know a robin
From a cuckoo or a crow
Will hear the little sparrows
Chirping in the snow.

When All the World Is Full of Snow
by N. M. Bodecker

I never know
just where to go,
when all the world
is full of snow.

I do not want
to make a track,
not even
to the shed and back.

I only want
to watch and wait,
while snow moths settle
on the gate,

and swarming frost flakes
fill the trees
with billions
of albino bees.

I only want
myself to be
as silent as
a winter tree,

to hear the swirling
stillness grow,
when all the world
is full of snow.

Winter Moon
by Langston Hughes

How thin and sharp is the moon tonight!
How thin and sharp and ghostly white
Is the slim curved crook of the moon tonight!

A Kite

author unknown

I often sit and wish that I
Could be a kite up in the sky,
And ride upon the breeze and go
Whichever way I chanced to blow.

The Wind

by Robert Louis Stevenson

I saw you toss the kites on high
And blow the birds about the sky;
And all around I heard you pass,
Like ladies' skirts across the grass—
 O wind, a-blowing all day long,
 O wind, that sings so loud a song!

I saw the different things you did,
But always you yourself you hid.
I felt you push, I heard you call,
I could not see yourself at all—
 O wind, a-blowing all day long,
 O wind, that sings so loud a song!

O you that are so strong and cold,
O blower, are you young or old?
Are you a beast of field and tree,
Or just a stronger child than me?
 O wind, a-blowing all day long,
 O wind, that sings so loud a song!

Who Has Seen the Wind?

by Christina Rossetti

Who has seen the wind?
 Neither I nor you;
But when the leaves hang trembling,
 The wind is passing through.

Who has seen the wind?
 Neither you nor I;
But when the trees
 Bow down their heads,
The wind is passing by.

Windy Nights

by Robert Louis Stevenson

Whenever the moon and stars are set,
  Whenever the wind is high,
All night long in the dark and wet,
  A man goes riding by.
Late in the night when the fires are out,
Why does he gallop and gallop about?

Whenever the trees are crying aloud,
  And ships are tossed at sea,
By, on the highway, low and loud,
  By at the gallop goes he:
By at the gallop he goes, and then
By he comes back at the gallop again.

Keep a Poem
in Your Pocket

by Beatrice Schenk de Regniers

Keep a poem in your pocket
and a picture in your head
and you'll never feel lonely
at night when you're in bed.

The little poem will sing to you
the little picture bring to you
a dozen dreams to dance to you
at night when you're in bed.

So—
Keep a picture in your pocket
and a poem in your head
and you'll never feel lonely
at night when you're in bed.

The wind
only
I am afraid of.
    a Chippewa Indian song

297

Illustration Acknowledgments

The publishers of *Childcraft* gratefully acknowledge the following artists, photographers, publishers, agencies, and corporations for illustrations in this volume. Page numbers refer to two-page spreads. All illustrations are the exclusive property of the publishers of *Childcraft* unless names are marked with an asterisk (*).

1:	*(top left)* Ron LeHew; *(top right)* Dennis Hockerman; *(bottom left)* Karen Loccisano; John Nez; *(bottom right)* Elise Primavera
6-13:	Diane Dawson
14-15:	Helen Oxenbury; Robert Byrd
16-25:	Betsy Day
26-27:	Linda Liefer
28:	Joan Podgorski
29:	Linda Liefer
31-38:	Marlene Ekman
40:	Robert Byrd
41-43:	Dennis Hockerman
44-53:	Arnold Lobel*
54-55:	Dennis Hockerman
56-70:	Crosby Bonsall*
72:	Linda Liefer
73:	Robert Byrd
74-75:	Dennis Hockerman
76-91:	John Nez
92-97:	Elise Primavera
98:	Robert Byrd

99:	Dennis Hockerman
100-101:	Dora Leder; Robert Byrd
102-116:	Joel Schick
118-123:	Linda Liefer
124-139:	Marlene Ekman
140-141:	Rodney Pate
142:	Dennis Hockerman
143:	Robert Byrd
144-150:	Mou-sien Tseng
151:	Robert Byrd
152-153:	Linda Liefer; Robert Byrd
154-165:	Barbara Lanza
166:	Robert Byrd
167:	Linda Liefer
168-169:	Marlene Ekman; Ron LeHew
170-179:	Karen Loccisano
180-181:	Joan Podgorski
182-183:	Karen Loccisano
184-185:	Joan Podgorski
186:	Ron LeHew
187:	Peter Geissler (Specs Art Agency)
188:	Joan Podgorski

189-203:	Jan Palmer
205:	Joan Podgorski
206-211:	Ron LeHew
212-231:	Robert McCloskey*
232-235:	Mou-sien Tseng
236:	Rodney Pate
237-249:	Peggy Fortnum*
251:	Marla Frazee
252-253:	Rodney Pate
254-262:	Karen Loccisano
264-265:	Joan Podgorski
266-269:	Karen Loccisano
270-271:	Joan Podgorski
272:	Karen Loccisano
274-275:	Marla Frazee
276-290:	Garth Williams*
291:	Rodney Pate
292-294:	Mou-sien Tseng
295:	Yoshi Miyake
296-297:	Mou-sien Tseng
Cover:	Elizabeth Miles

(*Acknowledgments continued from page 2*)

by Russell Hoban. Text copyright © 1964, 1972 by Russell Hoban. Reprinted by permission of Harper & Row, Publishers, Inc., and Faber & Faber Ltd. From *Dogs and Dragons, Trees and Dreams* by Karla Kuskin: Text only of the first stanza of "Counting," copyright © 1964 by Karla Kuskin; text only of "The Gold-Tinted Dragon," copyright © 1958 by Karla Kuskin; "I Woke Up This Morning," copyright © 1958 by Karla Kuskin; "Me," copyright © 1980 by Karla Kuskin; and text only of "Rules," copyright © 1962 by Karla Kuskin. Reprinted by permission of Harper & Row, Publishers, Inc. Text only of *I Should Have Stayed in Bed* by Joan M. Lexau. Text copyright © 1965 by Joan M. Lexau. Reprinted by permission of Harper & Row, Publishers, Inc. Published in Great Britain by World's Work Ltd. Text of "A Lost Button" and "A Swim" and 11 illustrations from *Frog and Toad Are Friends* by Arnold Lobel. Copyright © 1970 by Arnold Lobel. Reprinted by permission of Harper & Row, Publishers, Inc. Published in Great Britain by World's Work Ltd. "Daylight Saving Time" (text only) from *Wonderful Time* by Phyllis McGinley (J. B. Lippincott Company). Text copyright © 1965, 1966 by Phyllis McGinley. Reprinted by permission of Harper & Row, Publishers, Inc., and Curtis Brown Ltd. "The Dragon of Grindly Grun" and "Pie Problem" from *A Light in the Attic: Poems and Drawings of Shel Silverstein*. Copyright © 1981 by Snake Eye Music, Inc. Reprinted by permission of Harper & Row, Publishers, Inc., and Jonathan Cape Ltd. "Sick" and "Smart" from *Where the Sidewalk Ends: Poems and Drawings of Shel Silverstein*. Copyright © 1974 by Snake Eye Music, Inc. Reprinted by permission of Harper & Row, Publishers, Inc., and Edite Kroll. Text of "Christmas in the Little House" and selected illustrations from *Little House in the Big Woods* by Laura Ingalls Wilder. Pictures by Garth Williams. Text copyright 1932 by Laura Ingalls Wilder. Pictures copyright 1953 by Garth Williams; renewed 1981 by Garth Williams. Reprinted by permission of Harper & Row, Publishers, Inc., and Methuen Children's Books. Complete text of *Harry the Dirty Dog* by Gene Zion. Text copyright © 1956 by Eugene Zion. Reprinted by permission of Harper & Row, Publishers, Inc., and The Bodley Head. "People" (text only) from *All That Sunlight* by Charlotte Zolotow. Text copyright © 1967 by Charlotte Zolotow. Reprinted by permission of Harper & Row, Publishers, Inc.

Harper's Magazine: "The Ostrich Is a Silly Bird" by Mary E. Wilkins Freeman. Copyright © 1905 by *Harper's* Magazine. All rights reserved. Reprinted from the August 1905 issue by special permission.

Holt, Rinehart and Winston, Publishers: "Stopping by Woods on a Snowy Evening" from *The Poetry of Robert Frost* edited by Edward Connery Lathem. Copyright 1923, © 1969 by Holt, Rinehart and Winston. Copyright 1951 by Robert Frost. Reprinted by permission of Holt, Rinehart and Winston, Publishers; Jonathan Cape Ltd.; and the Estate of Robert Frost. *Sam, Bangs & Moonshine* written and illustrated by Evaline Ness. Copyright © 1966 by Evaline Ness. Reprinted by permission of Holt, Rinehart and Winston, Publishers.

Houghton Mifflin Company: "A Bear Called Paddington" from *A Bear Called Paddington* by Michael Bond. Copyright © 1958 by Michael Bond. Reprinted by permission of Houghton Mifflin Company, and Collins Publishers. "Guess" from *I Met a Man* by John Ciardi. Copyright © 1961 by John Ciardi. Reprinted by permission of Houghton Mifflin Company. "Alligator Pie" from *Alligator Pie* by Dennis Lee, copyright © 1974 by Dennis Lee, and "The Muddy Puddle" from *Garbage Delight* by Dennis Lee, copyright © 1977 by Dennis Lee. Reprinted by permission of Houghton Mifflin Company, and Macmillan of Canada, A Division of Gage Publishing Limited.

James Houston: Chippewa, Eastern Eskimo, Kiowa, Osage, Winnebago, Yaqui, and Yuma songs from *Songs of the Dream People: Chants and Images from the Indians and Eskimos of North America* edited and illustrated by James Houston.

Barbara Boyden Jordan: "Mud" by Polly Chase Boyden from *Child Life Magazine*. Copyright 1930, 1958 by Rand McNally & Company.

Dennis Lee: "Freddy" by Dennis Lee from *Jelly Belly* (Macmillan of Canada, A Division of Gage Publishing).

Ray Lincoln Literary Agency: "Eat-It-All Elaine" from *Don't Ever Cross a Crocodile* by Kaye Starbird. Copyright © 1963 by Kaye Starbird. By permission of Ray Lincoln Literary Agency, 4 Surrey Road, Melrose Park, Pa. 19126 U.S.A.

Little, Brown and Company: "Song of the Train" from *One at a Time* by David McCord. Copyright 1952 by David McCord. By permission of Little, Brown and Company.

Macmillan Publishing Company, Inc.: "The Sea Gull Curves His Wings" from *Summer Green* by Elizabeth Coatsworth. Copyright 1947 by Macmillan Publishing Co., Inc.; renewed 1975 by Elizabeth Coatsworth Beston. "Something Told the Wild Geese" from *Branches Green* by Rachel Field. Copyright 1934 by Macmillan Publishing Co., Inc.; renewed 1962 by Arthur S. Pederson. "The Moon's the North Wind's Cooky" from *Collected Poems* by Vachel Lindsay. Copyright 1914 by Macmillan Publishing Co., Inc.; renewed 1942 by Elizabeth C. Lindsay. "Night" and "The Falling Star" from *Collected Poems* by Sara

Teasdale. Copyright 1930 by Sara Teasdale Filsinger; renewed 1958 by Guaranty Trust Co. All reprinted with permission of Macmillan Publishing Company. *Abu Ali: Three Tales from the Middle East* by Dorothy O. Van Woerkom. Text copyright © 1976 by Dorothy O. Van Woerkom. Reprinted by arrangement with Macmillan Publishing Company. Published in Great Britain by World's Work Ltd.

Eve Merriam: "Quibble" from *There Is No Rhyme for Silver* by Eve Merriam, copyright © 1962 by Eve Merriam, and "Sing a Song of Subways" from *The Inner City Mother Goose* by Eve Merriam, copyright © 1969 by Eve Merriam. Used by permission of the author. All rights reserved.

William Morrow & Company, Inc.: "The Night of the Jack-O'-Lantern" from *Ramona and Her Father* by Beverly Cleary. Copyright © 1977 by Beverly Cleary. By permission of William Morrow & Company, and Hamish Hamilton Ltd., the British publishers. Complete text of *Teach Us, Amelia Bedelia* by Peggy Parish. Copyright © 1977 by Margaret Parish. By permission of Greenwillow Books (A Division of William Morrow & Company). Published in Great Britain by World's Work Ltd. "No Girls Allowed" from *Rolling Harvey Down the Hill* by Jack Prelutsky, copyright © 1980 by Jack Prelutsky, and "Toucans Two" from *Zoo Doings* by Jack Prelutsky, copyright © 1970, 1983 by Jack Prelutsky. By permission of Greenwillow Books (A Division of William Morrow & Co.).

Effie Lee Newsome: "Quoits."

The Putnam Publishing Group: "My Nose" by Dorothy Aldis. Reprinted by permission of G. P. Putnam's Sons from *All Together*. Copyright 1925-1928, 1934, 1939, 1952; copyright renewed 1953-1956, 1962, 1967 by Dorothy Aldis. Copyright © 1980 by Roy E. Porter.

Random House, Inc.: "The Frog" and "The Vulture" from *Cautionary Verses* by Hilaire Belloc. Published 1941 by Alfred A. Knopf, Inc. Reprinted by permission of Alfred A. Knopf, Inc., and Gerald Duckworth & Co. Ltd. "Winter Moon" from *Selected Poems of Langston Hughes*. Copyright © 1926 by Alfred A. Knopf, Inc.; renewed 1954 by Langston Hughes. Reprinted by permission of the publisher. "They've All Gone South" from *Listen—the Birds* by Mary Britton Miller. Copyright © 1961 by Pantheon Books, Inc. Reprinted by permission of Pantheon Books, a division of Random House, Inc. *Mother, Mother, I Want Another* by Maria Polushkin, illustrated by Diane Dawson. Text copyright © 1978 by Maria Polushkin. Illustrations copyright © 1978 by Diane Dawson. Reprinted by permission of Crown Publishers, Inc. *A Thousand Pails of Water* by Ronald Roy. Copyright © 1978 by Ronald Roy. Reprinted by permission of Alfred A. Knopf, Inc. "My Little Sister" from *All on a Summer's Day* by William Wise. Copyright © 1971 by William Wise. Reprinted by permission of Pantheon Books, a division of Random House, Inc., and Curtis Brown, Ltd.

Marian Reiner: "The Sun Is Stuck" from *A Crazy Flight and Other Poems* by Myra Cohn Livingston, copyright © 1969 by Myra Cohn Livingston, and "Whispers" from *Whispers and Other Poems* by Myra Cohn Livingston, copyright © 1958 by Myra Cohn Livingston. Reprinted by permission of Marian Reiner for the author.

Charles Scribner's Sons: "Amelia Mixed the Mustard" by A. E. Housman from *My Brother, A. E. Housman* by Laurence Housman. Copyright 1937, 1938 by Laurence Housman; copyrights renewed (New York: Charles Scribner's Sons, 1938). Reprinted by permission of Charles Scribner's Sons, The Society of Authors as the literary representative of the Estate of A. E. Housman, and Jonathan Cape Ltd., publishers of Housman's *Collected Poems*.

Sheed & Ward: "Daddy Fell Into the Pond" from *Daddy Fell Into the Pond and Other Poems* by Alfred Noyes. Used with permission of Sheed & Ward, 115 E. Armour Blvd., Kansas City, MO.

Simon & Schuster, Inc.: "The Slithergadee" from *Don't Bump the Glump*. Copyright © 1964 by Shel Silverstein. Reprinted by permission of Simon & Schuster, Inc.

Smithsonian Institution Press: "Chippewa Song" from *Chippewa Music II* by Frances Densmore. By permission of the Smithsonian Institution Press. Smithsonian Institution, Washington, D.C., 1913.

Arnold Spilka: "I Saw a Little Girl I Hate" from *A Rumbudgin of Nonsense* by Arnold Spilka. Published by Charles Scribner's Sons © 1970. Permission granted by the author.

Viking Penguin Inc.: A selection, abridged, from *Pippi Longstocking* by Astrid Lindgren. Translated by Florence Lamborn. Copyright 1950 by The Viking Press, Inc. Copyright renewed © 1978 by Viking Press, Inc. Reprinted by permission of Viking Penguin Inc. The complete text and selected illustrations from *One Morning in Maine* by Robert McCloskey. Copyright renewed © 1980 by Robert McCloskey. Reprinted by arrangement with Viking Penguin Inc. "Firefly" from *Under the Tree* by Elizabeth Madox Roberts. Copyright 1922 by B. W. Huebsch Inc.; renewed 1950 by Ivor S. Roberts. Copyright 1930 by The Viking Press, Inc.; renewed © 1958 by Ivor S. Roberts and The Viking Press, Inc. Reprinted by permission of Viking Penguin Inc.

Author Index

This index is divided into two parts: **Authors of Stories** and **Authors of Poems.** If you know the name of the author you are looking for, use this index. You can also find a story or a poem by using the **Title Index** or a poem by using the **First-Line Index.** For more stories and poems, see the indexes in volumes 1 and 3. For stories and poems in all other volumes, see the entries **poems and rhymes, poets,** and **stories** in the General Index in Volume 15.

Authors of Stories

Blume, Judy
Family Dog, The, 124
Bond, Michael
Bear Called Paddington, A, 237
Bonsall, Crosby
Case of the Cat's Meow, The, 56

Cleary, Beverly
Night of the Jack-O'-Lantern, The, 188

Lexau, Joan M.
I Should Have Stayed in Bed, 16

Lindgren, Astrid
Pippi Goes to the Circus, 254
Lobel, Arnold
Frog and Toad, 44

McCloskey, Robert
One Morning in Maine, 212

Ness, Evaline
Sam, Bangs & Moonshine, 154

Parish, Peggy
Teach Us, Amelia Bedelia, 102
Polushkin, Maria
Mother, Mother, I Want Another, 6

Roy, Ronald
Thousand Pails of Water, A, 144

Sobol, Donald J.
Encyclopedia Brown, 170

Van Woerkom, Dorothy O.
Abu Ali: Three Tales of the Middle East, 30

Wilder, Laura Ingalls
Christmas in the Little House, 276
Wiseman, Bernard
Riddles, The, 76

Zion, Gene
Harry the Dirty Dog, 92

Authors of Poems

Aldis, Dorothy
My Nose, 28
Allen, Marie Louise
First Snow, 294
author unknown
Algy Met a Bear, 40
Chippewa Indian song, A, 291, 297
Eastern Eskimo Song, An, 153
Eensy, Weensy Spider, The, 151
Fox Went Out on a Chilly Night, The, 118
I Asked My Mother, 73
I Eat My Peas with Honey, 143
I Know an Old Lady Who Swallowed a Fly, 206
I Love You, 15
I Met a Man, 139
Kiowa Indian Song, A, 153
Kite, A, 296
Man Is a Fool, 41
Osage Indian Song, An, 235
Question, 15
Sea, The, 152
Throughout the World, 28
To Be Answered in Our Next Issue, 187

Toot! Toot!, 40
Yaqui Indian Song, A, 151
Yuma Indian Song, A, 235

Bacmeister, Rhoda W.
Galoshes, 100
Belloc, Hilaire
Frog, The, 153
Vulture, The, 143
Bennett, Rowena Bastin
End-of-Summer Poem, 293
Bodecker, N. M.
When All the World Is Full of Snow, 295
Boyden, Polly Chase
Mud, 101
Brooks, Gwendolyn
Rudolph Is Tired of the City, 253
Vern, 99
Burgess, Gelett
Table Manners, 142

Chute, Marchette
Spring Rain, 151
Ciardi, John
Guess, 72
How to Tell a Tiger, 73
Mummy Slept Late and Daddy Fixed Breakfast, 274

Coatsworth, Elizabeth
Sea Gull, 152

De Regniers, Beatrice Schenk
Keep a Poem in Your Pocket, 297
Dickinson, Emily
Autumn, 292

Farjeon, Eleanor
Bedtime, 166
Night Will Never Stay, The, 234
Field, Rachel
If Once You Have Slept on an Island, 233
Something Told the Wild Geese, 292
Fisher, Aileen
June!, 291
Fraser, Kathleen
Wrestling, 54
Freeman, Mary E. Wilkins
Ostrich Is a Silly Bird, The, 73
Frost, Robert
Stopping by Woods on a Snowy Evening, 294

Hoban, Russell
Homework, 187
Stupid Old Myself, 29

Title Index

This index is divided into two parts: **Titles of Stories** and **Titles of Poems.** If you know the the title of the story or poem you are looking for, use this index. You can also find a story or a poem by using the **Author Index** or a poem by using the **First-Line Index.** For more stories and poems, see the indexes in volumes 1 and 3. For stories and poems in all other volumes, see the entries **poems and rhymes, poets,** and **stories** in the General Index in Volume 15.

Titles of Stories

Titles of Poems

First-Line Index to Poems

Use this index to find a poem if you know only the first line of the poem.
You can also find a poem by using the **Author Index** or the **Title Index**.
For more poems, see the indexes in volumes 1 and 3. For poems in all
other volumes, see the entries **poems and rhymes** and **poets** in the
General Index in Volume 15.